Penguin Education
Penguin English Project Stage One

Things Working
Edited by Penny Blackie

Chairman: Patrick Radley

Other Worlds
Edited by Donald Ball

Things Working
Edited by Penny Blackie

Family and School
Edited by David Jackson

Ventures
Edited by Elwyn Rowlands

I Took my Mind a Walk
Edited by George Sanders

Creatures Moving
Edited by Geoffrey Summerfield

Penguin English Projec

Edited by Penny Blackie

tage One Things Working

Penguin Books

Penguin Books Ltd, Harmondsworth,
Middlesex, England
Penguin Books Australia Ltd,
Ringwood, Victoria, Australia

First published 1970
Reprinted 1971
This selection copyright © Penny Blackie, 1970

Set in Monophoto Ehrhardt by
Oliver Burridge Filmsetting Ltd, Crawley, England
Printed in Great Britain by
Ebenezer Baylis & Son, Ltd., Worcester

Contents

Wings

We have
a microscopic anatomy
of the whale
this
gives
Man
assurance

William Carlos Williams

We have
a map of the universe
for microbes,
we have
a map of a microbe
for the universe.

We have
a Grand Master of chess
made of electronic circuits.

But above all
we have
the ability
to sort peas,
to cup water in our hands,
to seek
the right screw
under the sofa
for hours.

This
gives us
wings.

*Translated from the
Czech by George Theiner*
Miroslav Holub

9

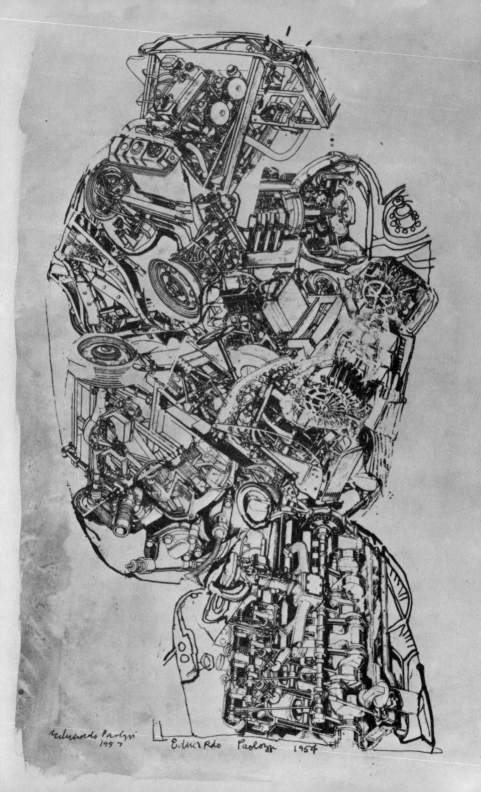

Who do you think you are
and where do you think you came from?
From toenails to the hair of your head you are
mixed of the earth, of the air,
Of compounds equal to the burning gold and ame-
thyst lights of the Mountains of the Blood of
Christ at Santa Fé.
Listen to the laboratory man tell what you are
made of, man, listen while he takes you apart.
Weighing 150 pounds you hold 3,500 cubic feet of
gas – oxygen, hydrogen, nitrogen.
From the 22 pounds and 10 ounces of carbon in
you is the filling for 9,000 lead pencils.
In your blood are 50 grains of iron and in the rest
of your frame enough iron to make a spike
that would hold your weight.
From your 50 ounces of phosphorus could be made
800,000 matches and elsewhere in your physical
premises are hidden 60 lumps of sugar, 20 tea-
spoons of salt, 38 quarts of water, two ounces
of lime, and scatterings of starch, chloride of
potash, magnesium, sulphur, hydrochloric acid.

You are a walking drug store and also a cosmos and
illusion   a phantasmagoria treading a lonesome valley,
one of the people, one of the minions and
masses   myrmidons who would like an answer to the
question, 'Who and what are you?'
One of the people seeing sun, fog, zero weather,
seeing fire, flood, famine, having meditations
On fish, birds, leaves, seeds,
Skins and shells emptied of living form,
The beautiful legs of Kentucky thoroughbreds
Carl Sandburg   And the patience of army mules.

I Like That Stuff
Lovers lie around in it.
Broken glass is found in it
Grass
I like that stuff

Tuna fish get trapped in it
Legs come wrapped in it
Nylon
I like that stuff

Eskimos and tramps chew it
Madame Tussaud gave status to it
Wax
I like that stuff

Elephants get sprayed with it
Scotch is made with it
Water
I like that stuff

Clergy are dumbfounded by it
Bones are surrounded by it
Flesh
I like that stuff

Harps are strung with it
Mattresses are sprung with it
Wire
I like that stuff

Carpenters make cots of it
Undertakers use lots of it
Wood
I like that stuff

Cigarettes are lit by it
Pensioners are happy when they sit by it
Fire
I like that stuff

Dankworth's alto is made of it, most of it,
Scoobdedoo is composed of it
Plastic
I like that stuff

Man made fibres and raw materials
Old rolled gold and breakfast cereals
Platinum linoleum
I like that stuff

Skin on my hands
Hair on my head
Toenails on my feet
And linen on my bed

Well I like that stuff
Yes I like that stuff
The earth
Is made of earth
Adrian Mitchell And I like that stuff

A View of Things what I love about dormice is their size
what I hate about rain is its sneer
what I love about the Bratach Gorm is its unflappability
what I hate about scent is its smell
what I love about newspapers is their etaoin shrdl
what I hate about philosophy is its pursed lip
what I love about Rory is his old grouse
what I hate about Pam is her pinkie
what I love about semi-precious stones is their preciousness
what I hate about diamonds is their mink
what I love about poetry is its ion engine
what I hate about hogs is their setae
what I love about love is its porridge-spoon
what I hate about hate is its eyes
what I love about hate is its salts
what I hate about love is its dog
what I love about Hank is his string vest
what I hate about the twins is their three gloves
what I love about Mabel is her teeter
what I hate about gooseberries is their look, feel, smell, and taste
what I love about the world is its shape
what I hate about a gun is its lock, stock, and barrel
what I love about bacon-and-eggs is its predictability
what I hate about derelict buildings is their reluctance to
    disintegrate
what I love about a cloud is its unpredictability
what I hate about you, chum, is your china
Edwin Morgan what I love about many waters is their inability to quench love

The sun had just begun to shine on the tent wall when I was woken by people moving about outside. It was the twelve long-ears who had come over from the cave to look at the statue and the problem that faced them. The largest statue at Anakena was the broad fellow who lay with his nose in the soil just beside our tent. He was a strapping sturdy giant, nearly ten feet wide across the shoulders and weighing between twenty-five and thirty tons. That meant more than two tons to lift for each of the twelve men. It was not surprising that they stood in a circle round the giant scratching their heads, but they seemed to have confidence in the mayor, and he walked about and studied the colossus with perfect calm.

Chief engineer Olsen also scratched his neck, shook his head and laughed.

'Well, if the mayor can manage that devil, he'll be a helluva fellow.'

'He'll never do it.'

'No, never!'

In the first place the giant lay at the foot of the wall with his head far down a slope, in addition he lay with his base four yards from the great slab on which he had originally stood. The mayor showed us some nasty little stones which he said had been wedged under the slab by the short-ears when they upset the statues.

Then he began to organize the work, as surely and calmly as if he had never done anything else. His only implements were three round poles, which he later reduced to two, a quantity of boulders and a few big stones which the men had collected in the vicinity. Even though the island is treeless today, apart from a few newly-planted clumps of eucalyptus, trees have always grown round the crater lake down in Rano Kao. There the first explorers found woods of *toro miro* and hibiscus, so the three wooden poles lay well within the scope of the permissible.

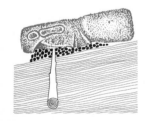

The figure had its face buried deep in the earth, but the men got the tips of their poles in underneath it, and while three or four men hung and heaved at the farthest end of each pole, the mayor lay flat on his stomach and pushed small stones under the huge face. Occasionally we saw a faint suggestion of movement in the giant when the eleven men got an extra good heave on the ends of their poles, but otherwise nothing happened except that the mayor lay there on his stomach

grubbing about with his stones. But the hours passed, and the stones he moved out and shoved in became larger and larger. When evening came the giant's head had been lifted a good three feet from the ground, while the space beneath was packed tight with stones.

Next day one of the poles was discarded as unnecessary, and five men assembled at each of the others. The mayor set his youngest brother to push the stones in under the statue: he himself stood up on the *ahu* wall with arms outstretched like the conductor of an orchestra, beating the air in time as he shouted concise orders to the men.

platform *or* plinth

'*Etahi, erua, etoru!* One, two, three! One, two, three! Hold on, push under! Once more! One, two, three! One, two, three!'

That day they pushed both poles under the right side of the giant. He tilted imperceptibly: but the imperceptible became millimetres and millimetres became inches which became feet. Then the two poles were moved over to the left side of the giant: this was treated in the same way as the right, and it too tilted up slowly, while all the time countless stones were carefully pushed in and arranged underneath. After that they turned back to the right side, then to the left again, and the right, and the left. And the statue rose steadily, still lying in a horizontal position on an ever rising heap of stones.

On the ninth day the huge figure stretched on its stomach on the top of an elaborately built tower the highest side of which was nearly twelve feet above the slope. It was quite uncanny to see this giant of nearly thirty tons lying stretched out up there, a whole man's height above the tops of our heads. The ten men could no longer reach the poles on which they hauled: they just hung dangling from ropes which were made fast to the ends. And still the giant had not begun to slant towards a standing position: we had not yet had a glimpse of the face of the figure as it lay on its stomach with the whole of its front hidden in the compact stone tower.

This looked deadly dangerous. Anette was no longer allowed to push her pram up to the statue with pebbles for the mayor. Now only the big strong men came staggering along barefoot like Neanderthal men with heavy boulders in their arms. The mayor was extremely careful, checking the position of every stone: the weight of the colossus was so great that some of the stones cracked under the pressure like lumps of sugar. A single careless placing could mean catastrophe. But it all had been thoroughly thought out, every little move was precisely and logically calculated. We stood with our hearts in our mouths as we saw the men pushing their bare toes in between the stones while clambering up the tower with more big blocks to be placed in position. Every single man was on the alert, and the mayor did not relax for a second. He held all the threads together and did not utter an unnecessary word. We had not known this side of him: we knew him in everyday life as a rather tiresome buffoon, a boaster and a bore, by no means popular among the men in the camp on account of his bragging and the shameless prices he put on his wood-carvings, though they were by far the best in the island. But now he was calm and assured, a born organizer and something of a practical genius. We began to see him with different eyes.

On the tenth day the statue lay at its highest. Imperceptibly the long-ears began to jerk it, feet foremost, in the direction of the *ahu* on which it was to stand.

On the eleventh day they began to raise the giant into a standing position by building the stones up even higher, but only under the face and chest.

On the seventeenth day a shrivelled old woman suddenly appeared among the long-ears. Together with the mayor she laid a semi-circle of stones as large as eggs at a certain distance in front of the statue's foot, on the great slab on which the giant was now beginning to fumble for a foothold. This was preventive magic. The statue was now standing at a dangerously sharp angle and there was imminent danger of its slipping forward of its own weight and rolling down the steep wall of the *ahu* towards the beach. Quite apart from a slip of this kind, it could also capsize in any direction when it was suddenly tilted off the tower and on to its own base. Accordingly the mayor tied a rope round the giant's forehead, and this was made fast to stakes in the ground on all four sides.

Then the eighteenth working day came. While some hauled on a rope down towards the beach and others held fast to another twisted round a post in the middle of the camp, the last cautious jerks with a wooden pole began. Suddenly the giant began to move quite visibly and the orders rang out:

'Hold on! Hold on!'

The giant rose in all his might and began to tilt upright, the tower was left standing without a counterpoise, a rumbling and sliding of stones began, and great blocks came crashing down on top of one another in a cloud of smoke and dust. But the colossus only wobbled and came quietly to rest in an upright position. There it stood, stiff and broad-shouldered, gazing out over the camp, unaffected by the change of scene since last it stood on the same foundation looking across the same temple square. The giant bulked so huge that the whole landscape was changed. The broad back was a landmark which could be seen far out to sea. We who lay in the tents at the foot of the wall and in the shadow of the giant's broad countenance no longer felt ourselves quite at home on Hotu Matua's old site. Wherever we went we saw the broad head close to us, towering over all the tent-tops like an old Norse mountain troll. When we moved about in the camp at night, the burly ogre seemed to come rolling forward out of the starry sky ready to strike over the green glowing tents in the darkness.

Aku Aku
Thor Heyerdahl

For the first time for hundreds of years one of the Easter Island giants stood in his place on the top of an *ahu*.

Plastecine Sculpture　　One of the things I love to make is sculptures. I am very keen on art but I sometimes get bored of always making images of three dimensional objects on a two dimensional surface. Paintings can sometimes look very real, but that is the only way in which they resemble the objects, they don't feel real, they have no depth. When I look at a beautiful painting of a landscape I always want to walk into it, to get inside it as if it were real. When I see a lovely painting of a face or something soft, fur or feathers or even something hard and rugged like stone the texture seems so real, but when I touch it to see if it really feels like that I am always disappointed.

A few weeks ago I decided to make something that felt real as well as looking real, something that had depth in it and didn't deceive the eye as paintings and drawings do. I was going to make a sculpture of a face, not just any face but the face of Esther Ofarim one of a pair of pop stars whom I like very much. I was going to make it by using photos of her as well as sketches. As I had no other material but small pieces of plastecine (which belong to my sister) it had to be quite small, about two inches long by one and a half inches broad. At first I had planned to make the face only, but then I decided that it would look a little strange if I gave Mrs Wignall half a head for art homework so then I decided to make a bust. I could see, even before I started, that this was going to be quite a task which would need delicate skill. I was going to do the face bit first and then tack it onto the rest of the head, neck and shoulders.

When I looked at Esther's photos a great 'wave' of inspiration came over me and I felt really excited about making her sculpture. That night I enthusiastically dreamed of my creation to be. I thought how beautiful it would be, how lovely the face would be, looking exactly like Esther, and the eyes, how gorgeous, clear and shining, just like real eyes. (I had even previously 'nicked' three pins with round, black shiny heads from our Physics lesson for her eyes. I took the third one as a spare just in case I lost one.) I was also going to give Esther real hair, fortunately her hair is about the same colour as mine and I had tons of hair which I had cut off last year kept in plastic bags. I was going to make her a wig and also I wanted to give her hair copper highlights with the copper poster paint that Mr Wysocki had lent me. Mr Wysocki's paints were going to come in very handy I could see, because I was going to make the face out of a greeny-yellow colour of plastecine, and I would obviously have to paint over it skin colour. I had planned every last detail of the sculpture, the lips were to be orange-pink and I was considering buying some clear colourless nail varnish to brush over them to make them shiny. I was so keen on making the sculpture perfect that I was even thinking of putting in tiny hairs for the eyebrows, but I changed my mind later thinking that this would be going a bit too far.

I began to make the sculpture using my fingers and a nail file but to my dismay it was terribly slow work and after about two and a half hours of delicate moulding, I found that the face had hardly progressed at all from the basic shape that I had started from. I found plastecine to be an awfully difficult material to work with, because it is so flexible and elastic, as soon as you make one indentation it pushes something else out of shape and so you are undoing and redoing your work all the time, virtually getting nowhere. Well that first attempt failed miserably, nothing seemed to go right, it certainly wasn't as easy as I had expected. In the end after having spent most of my holidays on it, I gave it up, and squashed it into a round ball again.

It's a strange sensation destroying something that you have put so much valuable energy and time into, completely transfiguring some beloved article, destroying a piece of work which has taken you so long in one blow which only lasts a few seconds. It was sad seeing those crushed features being twisted and distorted into a mess by the same hands which had given their form so much patience and loving care. But I had to do it because I had no more plastecine except that little lump.

After my first failure I felt rather discouraged but I wasn't going to give up so easily, so a few days later I began to model another Esther, this time it was much better. I began with the basic shape of the skeleton, adding and subtracting to it. I put two big pearls in the eye sockets to keep their shape. The thing I found most difficult to do was the nose. When I tried to cut out the nostrils the plastecine went funny, all jagged and the lips were too fat. One thing that also hindered me was that I had no photos of Esther's profile so I had no idea what it was like, so I just had to make vague guesses.

Well, after about another week the face was nearly completed and I was just adding the finishing touches and making sure

that everything was the right shape and size. I did this by checking it in a mirror to make sure that it was symmetrical but to my surprise I found many great errors. I checked it also by tilting it at different angles to the light and looking at its shadow on the wall. It was not terribly good, not as good

as I would have liked, not quite what I had expected, but anyway I said that it would have to do. I was just smoothing down the little bumps on the surface with my finger tips, gently and hollowing out the eyes, then I casually put it down on the bed beside me where I was sitting. I got up and went away, for some reason, and came back again to finish it off. When I got back I couldn't find it, I sat down on the bed to have a look but a few seconds later to my horror I found that I was sitting on it.

As I picked the plastecine face up I just couldn't bear to look at it, I hid my eyes with my hand anxiously muttering 'No! Oh No!' . . . The nose was as flat as a pancake, the eyes were squashed in like Frankenstein's and the mouth was a twisted mangle, unrecognizable.

I was so depressed at this and I kept confounding myself for my clumsiness. I thought I had given up now, but when I got some new pictures of Esther (with Abi) I was encouraged to try again.

This time it went miraculously, so I thought. After one afternoon I had done about half of the face, by the end of the week I had just about finished the face part. This time I didn't put any pearls in because they made things much more difficult. I tried also to remember not to make her nose too sharp or too round for Esther has a nose which can look sharp and round in photos so it was hard for me to decide which it really was. I had to make her lips thin but not too small and her cheekbones were high, but she still had a round kind of face in other pictures, and although I had about fifteen photos of her she looked so completely different in all of them that I couldn't decide what she really looked like.

I scraped and patted away night and day and at about 11 o'clock on Saturday night I was still at it. When I start to make something that I am enjoying I can't stop until I've finished. I find its just like chewing gum, when I chew it for a long time I hate to spit it out because my mouth feels so queer afterwards, so tired, but the longer I chew the tireder I get, it must be like taking a drug.

I fixed the rest of the head, neck and shoulders on with a lot of effort, I didn't have enough plastecine so I had to put a marble inside the head to save some space. I called this the brain.

The following day I was still shaping it and almost all day I was doing it. I started it in the morning and worked at it all day, unintentionally. The day crept by without my noticing it and at bedtime I just couldn't imagine where the day had gone,

it had seemed so short. Well, I decided that I would just finish
it off on Sunday and have the rest of the day free, but I found
that it took so long that Sunday was gone too before I hardly
even had time to think about anything else.

I stood the bust in the window sill as well as all the rest of my
tools and equipment and began to paint the face 'flesh' colour.
But when it was dry it turned out to be more like a salmon
pink. I painted the head part black and began to make the
wig. When I put the black eye make up on the eyes it really
did begin to look quite nice and I thought that even if I had
spent all weekend on it, it was going to be worthwhile after all.
I thought it really looked like an ancient Egyptian carving,
with its long curving neck and elf-like, highly domed skull,
although it wasn't half as good as I had hoped for I was quite
pleased with it.

But just as I was admiring it in the mirror and giving myself a
pat on the back, it toppled over and fell flat on its nose. The
paint was chipped off and the nose was completely flattened. I
tried frantically to squeeze it back into shape but as I did so
all the rest of the face was mutilated. I could feel my blood
getting hot, a feeling of defeat and desperation came over me
like a dousing of water. Gripped by a terrible rage, something
snapped inside me. I squeezed the plastecine with all my might
and slammed it down again and again on the window sill still
gritting my teeth, swearing and crying as I did so. I suddenly
looked at the mangled plastecine that had once been the face
and thought, between my tears, 'What have I done?' I felt so
tired and depressed. I thought I should finish it off. I stamped
it flat under my shoe and tore it into little lumps crying like a
howling dog. It was night time, 'Back to rotten old school in
the morning', I thought miserably. How I had longed for the
weekend and some rest all through the week, and now it had
all been wasted on that accursed thing.

I was as tired as a beaten-up rat in the morning, and I swore I
would never try to make another sculpture in all my life again.

But last Saturday I thought I would have another bash at it,
and I bought a small packet of putty. It was as soft as dough
and everytime I go near it the smell puts me right off so I
don't think that's going to be a success either. Now I just hope
that one day my Esther will be made eventually and that she
Age 14   will turn out as I first planned, I will never have any peace of
Alice McKeown   mind until I do make her – unfortunately I just can't give up.

Carving a Goldfish

The penknife glides through the polystyrene,
turning it to get a good angle.
Smoothly the oiled blade cuts
as my dad carves a goldfish.
All his face is screwed up.
He sees nothing but his moving hand,
and doesn't know I'm there.
Hands last night that were rough, big and clumsy
as the floorboards were torn up,
and thick cable cut to lay beneath.
Now, as I watch,
I wonder at the care of his delicate hands,
As a small perfect goldfish forms.

Ian Griffiths

Jug   The shale and water thrown together so-so first of all,
Then a potter's hand on the wheel and his fingers shaping
 the jug; out of the mud a mouth and a handle;
Slimpsy, loose and ready to fall at a touch, fire plays
 on it, slow fire coaxing all the water out of the shale mix.
Dipped in glaze more fire plays on it till a molasses lava
 runs in waves, rises and retreats, a varnish of volcanoes.
Take it now; out of mud now here is a mouth and handle;
 out of this now mothers will pour milk and maple syrup
corn syrup   and cider, vinegar, apple juice, and sorghum.
There is nothing proud about this; only one out of
 many; the potter's wheel slings them out and the
 fires harden them hours and hours thousands and thousands.
'Be good to me, put me down easy on the floors of the
 new concrete houses; I was poured out like a concrete
Carl Sandburg   house and baked in fire too.'

The Picket Fence

One time there was a picket fence
with space to gaze from hence to thence.

An architect who saw this sight
approached it suddenly one night,

removed the spaces from the fence,
and built of them a residence.

The picket fence stood there dumbfounded
with pickets wholly unsurrounded,

a view so loathsome and obscene,
the Senate had to intervene.

The architect, however, flew
To Afri- or Americoo.

*Translated from the
German by Max Knight*
**Christian
Morgenstern**

The Principle of the Helicopter

Translated from the Italian by E. McCurdy
Leonardo da Vinci

I say that if this instrument made with a helix is well made, that is to say, of flaxen linen, of which one has closed the pores with starch and is turned with great speed, the said helix is able to make a screw in the air, and to climb high. Take the example of a wide and thin ruler and directed violently into the air; you will see that your arm will be guided by the line of the edge of the said board. . . . One is able to make a little model of this of cardboard, whose axis should be of thin sheet-iron, twisted with force; on freeing this, it causes the helix to turn.

27

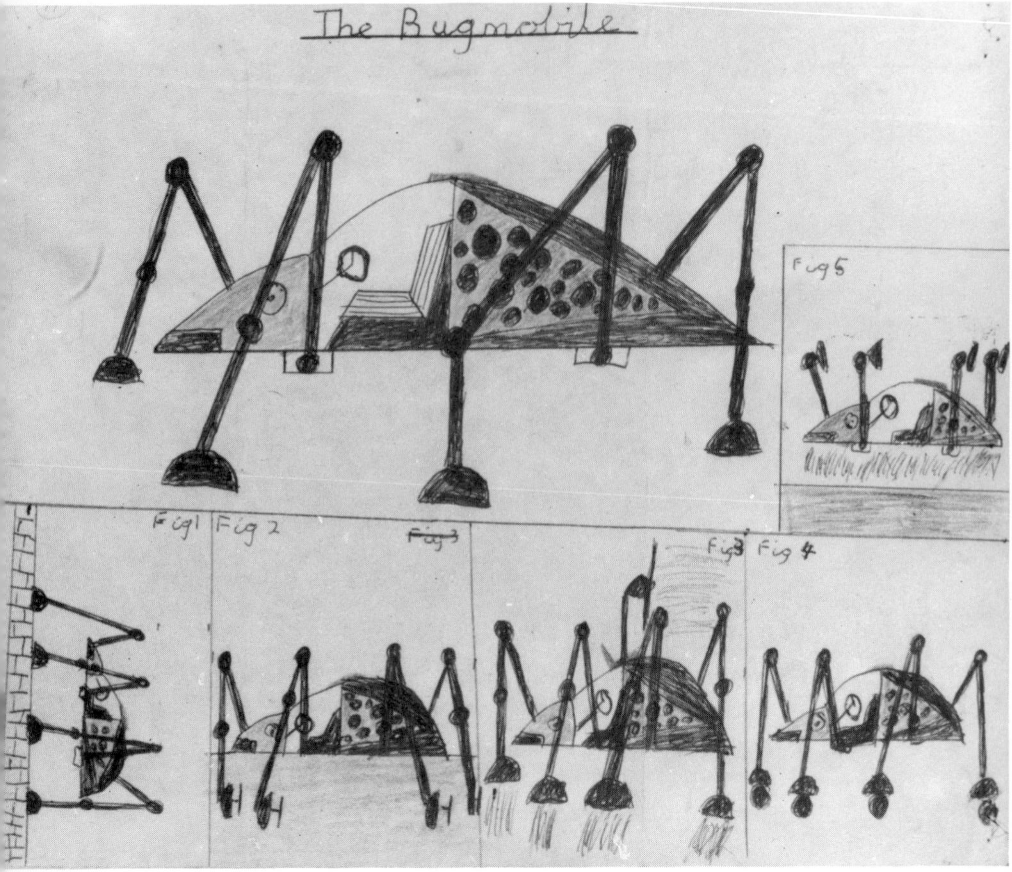

The Bugmobile

The Bugmobile

1 Suckers on feet allow it to move vertically.

2 It can become amphibious by fitting propellers to pads.

3 Lift is devised by air pressure from feet, thrust is devised by propeller coming out of roof, enabling it to become airborne.

4 Wheels fitted to legs enable it to move at high speeds for ordinary travel.

Age 11
David Karliner

5 By reversing legs vertically and withdrawing limbs it can move like a hovercraft.

A machine for travelling over rough ground.

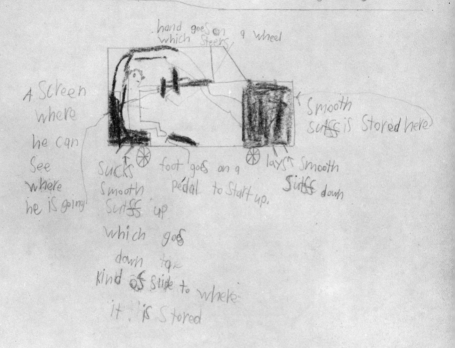

hand goes on a wheel
which steers

A screen where he can see where he is going

smooth stuff is stored here

sucks foot goes on a pedal to start up. lays smooth stuff down

smooth stuff up

which goes down the kind of slide to where it is stored

A Machine for Travelling over Rough Ground

Paul Tant

A brilliantly novel solution to conquering rough ground: get rid of it by spreading 'Smooth stuff' in front of the vehicle. 'Smooth stuff' is sucked up at the back, carried through a pipe to the front, stored, and laid down to fill in the bumps. (Edward de Bono)

In general I like:

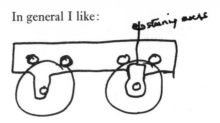

Large soft (very soft) tyres. Drive applied to land wheels via wheels driving *perimeter* of land wheels. Operates over wide range of terrain. Or tracked vehicle, or multi-axle:

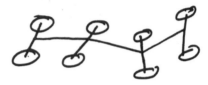

Multi-axle: if wheel size and profile are right it can probably claw up inclines or sudden steps better – however, the drive problems and chassis construction are considerable.

Carrying it all to an extreme, how about:

How does it stay upright? Gyro? Large counter-weight below axle? Trailing outrigger wheel and servo? How does it steer? Steers by having main (front) wheel in two sections and driving at different speeds – rear wheel swings on castor action.

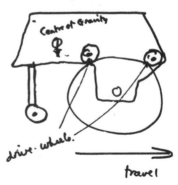

A. Gosling This should cover anything that isn't so steep that it slips back.

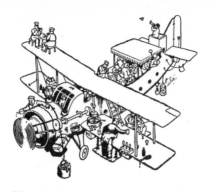

How to Find Heath Robinson

First I will give you this letter H. H-
old onto it carefully, because you see
it's attached by a long string to a kite
and now you must wind the kite in
and here it comes down, k first, then i,
then t, and now you must grab its tail
which is E – have you got it? Good.
Stuck to the tail you will find something
it caught from a tree on its journey down,
and this is important because it's an a-
corn. Throw away the corn, and you
have A. But watch the corn because
it's going to sprout and sprout and sprout
and you must wait for the last sprou-
t and catch it by the ear for T.
Tiptoe into the house, quietly.
Now you will see what you want at the end
of the bath. It is an H. Take it
off the tap, put it in your pocket,
turn on the tap, and before you can say
Jack, out it comes all piping hot
R, O, B, I, N, S, O, N –
rows of bubbles in neat strings of noodles.
Take them and hang them up to dry,
and in the morning gather them together,
and lay them down at the edge of the heath
which has grown from your letters while you slept.
Zap! Bingo! Pow! Eureka!
And there he is, with a chimney hat
and a gentle smile and a plumber's bag
and a home-made kite and a pot of tea
and a packet of corn, and he says 'Good-morning,
first I will give you this letter I. I . . . '

Edwin Morgan

Resuscitating stale railway scones for redistribution at the station buffets

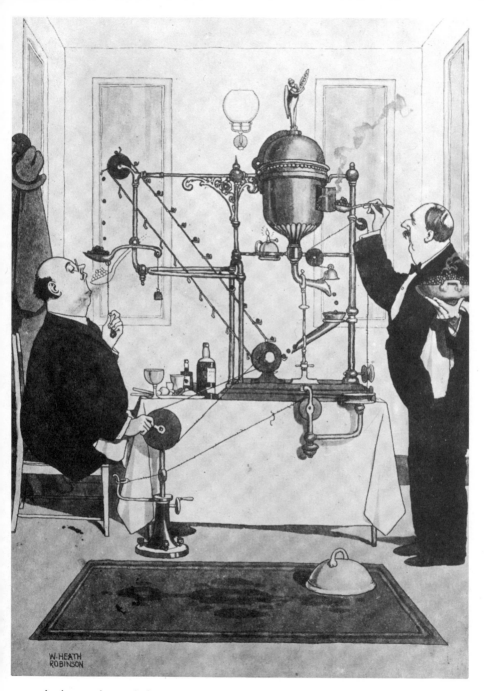

An interesting and elegant apparatus designed to overcome once for all the
difficulties of conveying green peas to the mouth

Some ingenious devices for use on chilly mornings

The subzeppmarinellin for making sure of your enemy

New Method of Locomotion

Anonymous

Our engraving shows a new mode of utilizing the principle of stilts for locomotion, which has been patented by Mr Samuel Davies. The action of propelling is that of skating on ice, and any forward figure that can be done on ice can be accomplished with ease by these machines. Each wheel is independent of the other, and backward travel is prevented by a mechanical action. An idea how to learn to ride them is given in the engraving. The balance is the first movement to be learnt. By pressing the thumbs on the brakes the wheels become fixed, by which means the learner can walk on them the same as on stilts. When the balance of walking is acquired, the learner may gradually let go the brake on one side for the wheel to move a little forward, then fix the brake on the wheel advanced, let go the brake on the opposite side, and advance that wheel a little in front of the other, always, however, taking care to brake the front wheel before advancing the hind one. By this means the action of the wheels moving under you is acquired, but it is advisable to go slowly to work at first. When the balance is lost it is best to jump off the machines and commence again, as the rider is not fixed in any way on the machine. The treadles are free to move with the toe or heel so that the control of the machines when in motion can be retarded by pressing the toe down, or the reverse, by pressing the heel down. The handles have the same effect: by throwing forward they retard the wheels, by placing them backward they assist the progress.

Sitting While Asleep

A very ingenious invention comes from Germany, which enables the user to rest as comfortably and safely as if lying on a bed, as it provides a rest for head, neck, back and elbow at the same time. The invention will be readily understood from our illustration, and it is claimed for it that the appliance is especially useful in the case of travelling for long distances by rail. It is also easily packed away in a small parcel, which can be carried in the pocket. It is claimed that by using the invention the traveller will hardly feel the shaking of the railway carriage, while he can at any time by means of a single turn change his position as he likes by leaning to the right or left, or sitting straight, but in any case there is a firm support for his head. The appliance is especially useful for asthmatic persons and those with chest complaints, and we understand that eminent German physicians speak most highly of the invention. The appliance is also used for sitting upright in bed, in which case it is fastened to a hook fixed in the ceiling.

As the price is moderate, this excellent invention should meet
with considerable support in this country. The inventor is
Anonymous   Mr P. Knüppelholz.

The Patent   The Patent Impulsoria, an ingenious invention introduced
Impulsoria at   from Italy by Signor Masserano, and demonstrated at the
Nine-Elms   Nine-Elms terminus of the South-Western Railway, applies
animal power to the working of railways. An artificial ground,
or platform, is caused by the movement of the horses' hooves
to actuate the leading wheels of the locomotive, thus propelling
the vehicle. By the movement of a lever the speed of the
vehicle may be varied, or it may even be reversed, regardless
Anonymous   of the speed, etc., of the animals.

Making a Door   After breakfast he hitched up Pet and Patty, and taking his axe he went to get timber for the door. Laura helped wash the dishes and make the beds, but that day Mary minded the baby. Laura helped Pa make the door. Mary watched, but Laura handed him his tools.

With the saw he sawed logs the right length for a door. He sawed shorter lengths for cross-pieces. Then with the axe he split the logs into slabs, and smoothed them nicely. He laid the long slabs together on the ground and placed the shorter slabs across them. Then with the auger he bored holes through the cross-pieces into the long slabs. Into every hole he drove a wooden peg that fitted tightly.

That made the door. It was a good oak door, solid and strong.

For the hinges he cut three long straps. One hinge was to be near the top of the door, one near the bottom, and one in the middle.

He fastened them first on the door, in this way: he laid a little piece of wood on the door, and bored a hole through it into the door. Then he doubled one end of a strap around the little piece of wood, and with his knife cut round holes through the strap. He laid the little piece of wood on the door again, with the strap doubled around it, and all the holes making one hole. Then Laura gave him a peg and the hammer, and he drove the peg into the hole. The peg went through the strap and the little piece of wood and through the strap again and into the door. That held the strap so that it couldn't get loose.

'I told you a fellow doesn't need nails!' Pa said.

When he had fastened the three hinges to the door, he set the door in the doorway. It fitted. Then he pegged strips of wood to the old slabs on either side of the doorway, to keep the door from swinging outward. He set the door in place again, and Laura stood against it to hold it there, while Pa fastened the hinges to the door-frame.

But before he did this he had made the latch on the door, because, of course, there must be some way to keep a door shut.

This was the way he made the latch: first he hewed a short, thick piece of oak. From one side of this, in the middle, he cut a wide deep notch. He pegged this stick to the inside of the

door, up and down and near the edge. He put the notched side against the door, so that the notch made a little slot.

Then he hewed and whittled a longer, smaller stick. This stick was small enough to slip easily through the slot. He slid one end of it through the slot, and he pegged the other end in the door.

But he did not peg it tightly. The peg was solid and firm in the door, but the hole in the stick was larger than the peg. The only thing that held the stick on the door was the slot.

This stick was the latch. It turned easily on the peg, and its loose end moved up and down in the slot. And the loose end of it was long enough to go through the slot and across the crack between the door and the wall, and to lie against the wall when the door was shut.

When Pa and Laura had hung the door in the doorway, Pa marked the spot on the wall where the end of the latch came. Over that spot he pegged to the wall a stout piece of oak. That held the latch against the wall, and the up-and-down strip held the latch in its slot against the door.

Nobody could break in without breaking the strong latch in two.

But there must be a way to lift the latch from the outside. So Pa made the latch-string. He cut it from a long strip of good leather. He tied one end to the latch, between the peg and the slot. Above the latch he bored a small hole through the door, and he pushed the end of the latch string through the hole.

Laura stood outside, and when the end of the latch-string came through the hole she took hold of it and pulled. She could pull it hard enough to lift the latch and let herself in.

The door was finished. It was strong and solid, made of thick oak with oak slabs across it, all pegged together with good stout pegs. The latch-string was out; if you wanted to come in, you pulled the latch-string. But if you were inside and wanted to keep anyone out, then you pulled the latch-string in through its hole and nobody could get in. There was no doorknob on that door, and there was no keyhole and no key. But it was a good door.

Little House
on the Prairie
Laura Ingalls Wilder

Shooting the Telly   So Japhet got off the bus, with a sinking heart, at the stop near the electric shop.

Slowly he walked up to the door. He paused at the window to look at a new TV that was on show there, working. There was Wimbledon tennis going on; normally Japhet took little interest in this, but now he stood gazing as if it were the most fascinating thing in the world. He was too deeply lost in his own thoughts to notice a figure draw near and stand by his side.

Slowly, reluctantly, he pushed open the door of the shop. A youth in a grey cotton dust-coat came forward to serve him.

'Yes, sir? Good afternoon.' They were always very polite in Cuthbertson's. There was even a carpet inside, most unusual for a village shop, and they had recently had a sound-proof box made where you could listen to gramophone records. There was a radio playing now, as well as the TV in the window; light tea-time music oozed round the electric fires and hair-dryers hanging on the glossy walls.

How could Japhet say, here, in these smooth and civilized surroundings, 'I've shot your telly'?

But that's just what he did say, in those very words.

The youth in the grey coat stared.

'I beg your pardon?' he said. Japhet told him again.

''Ang on,' said the astonished youth, forgetting his shop voice. He disappeared into the back quarters; Japhet waited for the terrible descent of Mr Cuthbertson, whom he had never actually seen . . . .

Japhet was certainly less scared than he had expected to be, as he told his story. He even put in what the Black Riders had been doing at the moment when he fired the shot.

Mr Cuthbertson listened attentively.

When the story was finished, he adjusted his spectacles, folded his arms and gave Japhet a long stare. Japhet quailed.

'Will it be terribly expensive?' he said. 'Will we have to pay for the whole set, or d'you think it could be repaired? I've got about fifteen shillings,' he added meekly, 'which I was saving up for something. But that doesn't matter now.'

Then Mr Cuthbertson said a most extraordinary thing. Of all the remarks Japhet might have expected, furious or threatening or just coldly stern, this remark wouldn't have occurred to him in the wildest dreams.

Mr Cuthbertson said: 'Did you get him?'

'Who?'

'The one you were shooting. Was it the thin one with the moustache?'

'No. The fat one with the scar,' said Japhet, dazed.

'I'd like to get that thin one,' Mr Cuthbertson said, narrowing his eyes. 'I reckon he's always the cause of the trouble. I wouldn't trust him from here to the shop next-door. I *hate* that thin one!' he added vehemently.

'Do you watch the Black Riders then?' Japhet wasn't sure if Mr Cuthbertson was pulling his leg, and would suddenly turn nasty after all.

'Regular,' said Mr Cuthbertson. 'Never miss. I like it when they go round that rock, don't you – my daughter, she says it's always the same old rock, every time, but she don't appreciate Westerns. Did you see the one where he stood up on top and lassoed 'em as they came galloping by underneath? That was good. But I wish you'd aimed at the thin one, though.'

'I'm afraid it went right through the glass,' said Japhet. 'The bullet must be inside somewhere.' He was beginning to feel that it was he who had to take charge of the situation. Mr Cuthbertson seemed slightly mad. Or to put it more kindly, he was even more of a TV enthusiast than Japhet himself – but between them they had a shot set on their hands.

'Well, we'll have to get the doctor to her, shan't we?' said Mr Cuthbertson. 'You tell your dad to keep the patient quiet till I get out there.'

'It can't be anything but quiet,' said Japhet. 'It's dead.' Mr Cuthbertson raised a large protesting paw.

The Day the Ceiling Fell Down
Jennifer Wayne

'Never use that word,' he said, 'while there's a current there's life. I'll be round tomorrow.'

Knob   Conceptually a blob,
the knob
is a smallish object which,
hitched
to a larger,
acts as verger.

It enables
us to gain access to drawers in end tables;
it shepherds
John Updike us into cupboards.

Glasses

I wear them. They help me. But I
Don't care for them. Two birds, steel hinges
Haunt each an edge of the small sky
My green eyes make. Rim-horn impinges
Upon my vision's furry fringes;
Faint dust collects upon the dry,
Unblinking shield behind which cringes
My naked, deprecated eye.

My gaze feels aimed. It is as if
Two manufactured beams had been
Lodged in my sockets – hollow, stiff,
And gray, like mailing tubes – and when
I pivot, vases topple down
From tabletops, and women frown.

John Updike

Spit Nolan   Spit Nolan was a pal of mine. He was a thin lad with a bony
face that was always pale, except for two rosy spots on his
cheekbones. He had quick brown eyes, short, wiry hair, rather
stooped shoulders, and we all knew that he had only one lung.
He had had a disease which in those days couldn't be cured,
unless you went away to Switzerland, which Spit certainly
couldn't afford. He wasn't sorry for himself in any way, and in
fact we envied him, because he never had to go to school.

Spit was the champion trolley-rider of Cotton Pocket; that
was the district in which we lived. He had a very good balance,
and sharp wits, and he was very brave, so that these qualities,
when added to his skill as a rider, meant that no other boy
could ever beat Spit on a trolley – and every lad had one.

Our trolleys were simple vehicles for getting a good ride
downhill at a fast speed. To make one you had to get a stout
piece of wood about five feet in length and eighteen inches
wide. Then you needed four wheels, preferably two pairs,
large ones for the back and smaller ones for the front.
However, since we bought our wheels from the scrapyard,
most trolleys had four odd wheels. Now you had to get a
poker and put it in the fire until it was red hot, and then burn
a hole through the wood at the front. Usually it would take
three or four attempts to get the hole bored through. Through
this hole you fitted the giant nut-and-bolt, which acted as a
swivel for the steering. Fastened to the nut was a strip of wood,
on to which the front axle was secured by bent nails. A piece
of rope tied to each end of the axle served for steering. Then
a knob of margarine had to be slanced out of the kitchen to
grease the wheels and bearings. Next you had to paint a name
on it: *Invincible* or *Dreadnought*, though it might be a motto:
Death before Dishonour or *Labour and Wait*. That done, you
then stuck your chest out, opened the back gate, and wheeled
your trolley out to face the critical eyes of the world.

Spit spent most mornings trying out new speed gadgets on his
trolley, or searching Enty's scrapyard for good wheels.
Afterwards he would go off and have a spin down Cemetery
Brew. This was a very steep road that led to the cemetery, and
it was very popular with trolley-drivers as it was the only
macadamized hill for miles around, all the others being
cobblestones for horse traffic. Spit used to lie in wait for a
coal-cart or other horse-drawn vehicle, then he would hitch
Egdam to the back to take it up the brew. *Egdam* was a name in
memory of a girl called Madge, whom he had once met at

Southport Sanatorium, where he had spent three happy weeks. Only I knew the meaning of it, for he had reversed the letters of her name to keep his love a secret.

It was the custom for lads to gather at the street corner on summer evenings and, trolleys parked at hand, discuss trolleying, road surfaces, and also show off any new gadgets. Then, when Spit gave the sign, we used to set off for Cemetery Brew. There was scarcely any evening traffic on the roads in those days, so that we could have a good practice before our evening race. Spit, the unbeaten champion, would inspect every trolley and rider, and allow a start which was reckoned on the size of the wheels and the weight of the rider. He was always the last in the line of starters, though no matter how long a start he gave it seemed impossible to beat him. He knew that road like the palm of his hand, every tiny lump or pothole, and he never came a cropper.

Among us he took things easy, but when occasion asked for it he would go all out. Once he had to meet a challenge from Ducker Smith, the champion of the Engine Row gang. On that occasion Spit borrowed a wheel from the baby's pram, removing one nearest the wall, so it wouldn't be missed, and confident he could replace it before his mother took baby out. And after fixing it to his trolley he made that ride on what was called the 'belly-down' style – that is, he lay full stretch on his stomach, so as to avoid wind resistance. Although Ducker got away with a flying start he had not that sensitive touch of Spit, and his frequent bumps and swerves lost him valuable inches, so that he lost the race with a good three lengths. Spit arrived home just in time to catch his mother as she was wheeling young Georgie off the doorstep, and if he had not made a dash for it the child would have fallen out as the pram overturned.

It happened that we were gathered at the street corner with our trolleys one evening when Ernie Haddock let out a hiccup of wonder: 'Hey, chaps, wot's Leslie got?'

We all turned our eyes on Leslie Duckett, the plump son of the local publican. He approached us on a brand-new trolley, propelled by flicks of his foot on the pavement. From a distance the thing had looked impressive, but now, when it came up among us, we were too dumbfounded to speak. Such a magnificent trolley had never been seen! The riding board was of solid oak, almost two inches thick; four new wheels with pneumatic tyres; a brake, a bell, a lamp, and a spotless steering-

cord. In front was a plate on which was the name in bold
lettering: *The British Queen.*

'It's called after the pub,' remarked Leslie. He tried to edge it
away from Spit's trolley, for it made *Egdam* appear horribly
insignificant. Voices had been stilled for a minute, but now
they broke out:

'Where'd it come from?'

'How much was it?'

'Who made it?'

Leslie tried to look modest. 'My dad had it specially made to
measure,' he said, 'by the gaffer of the Holt Engineering
Works.'

He was a nice lad, and now he wasn't sure whether to feel
proud or ashamed. The fact was, nobody had ever had a trolley
made by somebody else. Trolleys were swopped and so on, but
no lad had ever owned one that had been made by other hands.
We went quiet now, for Spit had calmly turned his attention to
it, and was examining *The British Queen* with his expert eye.
First he tilted it, so that one of the rear wheels was off the
ground, and after giving it a flick of the finger he listened
intently with his ear close to the hub.

'A beautiful ball-bearing race,' he remarked, 'it runs like silk.'
Next he turned his attention to the body. 'Grand piece of
timber, Leslie – though a trifle on the heavy side. It'll take
plenty of pulling up a brew.'

'I can pull it,' said Leslie, stiffening.

'You might find it a shade *front-heavy*,' went on Spit, 'which
means it'll be hard on the steering unless you keep it well oiled.'

'It's well made,' said Leslie. 'Eh, Spit?'

Spit nodded. 'Aye, all the bolts are counter-sunk,' he said,
'everything chamfered and fluted off to perfection. But – '

'But what?' asked Leslie.

'Do you want me to tell you?' asked Spit.

'Yes, I do,' answered Leslie.

'Well, it's got none of *you* in it,' said Spit.

'How do you mean?' says Leslie.

'Well, you haven't so much as given it a single tap with a hammer,' said Spit. 'That trolley will be a stranger to you to your dying day.'

'How come,' said Leslie, 'since I *own* it?'

Spit shook his head. 'You don't own it,' he said, in a quiet, solemn tone. 'You own nothing in this world except those things you have taken a hand in the making of, or else you've earned the money to buy them.'

Leslie sat down on *The British Queen* to think this one out. We all sat round, scratching our heads.

'You've forgotten to mention one thing,' said Ernie Haddock to Spit, 'what about the *speed*?'

'Going down a steep hill,' said Spit, 'she should hold the road well – an' with wheels like that she should certainly be able to shift some.'

'Think she could beat *Egdam*?' ventured Ernie.

'That,' said Spit, 'remains to be seen.'

Ernie gave a shout: 'A challenge race! *The British Queen* versus *Egdam*!'

'Not tonight,' said Leslie. 'I haven't got the proper feel of her yet.'

'What about Sunday morning?' I said.

Spit nodded. 'As good a time as any.'

Leslie agreed. 'By then,' he said in a challenging tone, 'I'll be able to handle her.'

Chattering like monkeys, eating bread, carrots, fruit, and bits of toffee, the entire gang of us made our way along the silent Sunday-morning streets for the big race at Cemetery Brew. We were split into two fairly equal sides.

Leslie, in his serge Sunday suit, walked ahead, with Ernie Haddock pulling *The British Queen*, and a bunch of supporters around. They were optimistic, for Leslie had easily outpaced every other trolley during the week, though as yet he had not run against Spit.

Spit was in the middle of the group behind, and I was pulling *Egdam* and keeping the pace easy, for I wanted Spit to keep

fresh. He walked in and out among us with an air of
imperturbability that, considering the occasion, seemed almost
godlike. It inspired a fanatical confidence in us. It was such that
Chick Dale, a curly-headed kid with a soft skin like a girl's, and
a nervous lisp, climbed up on to the spiked railings of the
cemetery, and, reaching out with his thin fingers, snatched a
yellow rose. He ran in front of Spit and thrust it into a small
hole in his jersey.

'I pwesent you with the wose of the winner!' he exclaimed.

'And I've a good mind to present you with a clout on the lug,'
replied Spit, 'for pinching a flower from a cemetery. An' what's
more, it's bad luck.' Seeing Chick's face, he relented. 'On
second thoughts, Chick, I'll wear it. Ee, wot a 'eavenly smell!'

Happily we went along, and Spit turned to a couple of lads at
the back. 'Hy, stop that whistling. Don't forget what day it is –
folk want their sleep out.'

A faint sweated glow had come over Spit's face when we
reached the top of the hill, but he was as majestically calm as
ever. Taking the bottle of cold water from his trolley seat, he
put it to his lips and rinsed out his mouth in the manner of a
boxer.

The two contestants were called together by Ernie.

'No bumpin' or borin',' he said.

They nodded.

'The winner,' he said, 'is the first who puts the nose of his
trolley past the cemetery gates.'

They nodded.

'Now, who,' he asked, 'is to be judge?'

Leslie looked at me. 'I've no objection to Bill,' he said. 'I know
he's straight.'

I hadn't realized I was, I thought, but by heck I will be!

'Ernie here,' said Spit, 'can be starter.'

With that Leslie and Spit shook hands.

'Fly down to them gates,' said Ernie to me. He had his father's
pigeon-timing watch in his hand. 'I'll be setting 'em off dead on
the stroke of ten o'clock.'

I hurried down to the gates. I looked back and saw the supporters lining themselves on either side of the road. Leslie was sitting upright on *The British Queen*. Spit was settling himself to ride belly-down. Ernie Haddock, handkerchief raised in the right hand, eye gazing down on the watch in the left, was counting them off – just like when he tossed one of his father's pigeons.

'Five – four – three – two – one – *Off!*'

Spit was away like a shot. That vigorous toe push sent him clean ahead of Leslie. A volley of shouts went up from his supporters, and groans from Leslie's. I saw Spit move straight to the middle of the road camber. Then I ran ahead to take up my position at the winning-post.

When I turned again I was surprised to see that Spit had not increased the lead. In fact, it seemed that Leslie had begun to gain on him. He had settled himself into a crouched position, and those perfect wheels combined with his extra weight were bringing him up with Spit. Not that it seemed possible he could ever catch him. For Spit, lying flat on his trolley, moving with a fine balance, gliding, as it were, over the rough patches, looked to me as though he were a bird that might suddenly open out its wings and fly clean into the air.

The runners along the side could no longer keep up with the trolleys. And now, as they skimmed past the halfway mark, and came to the very steepest part, there was no doubt that Leslie was gaining. Spit had never ridden better; he coaxed *Egdam* over the tricky parts, swayed with her, gave her her head, and guided her. Yet Leslie, clinging grimly to the steering-rope of *The British Queen*, and riding the rougher part of the road, was actually drawing level. Those beautiful ball-bearing wheels, engineer-made, encased in oil, were holding the road, and bringing Leslie along faster than spirit and skill could carry Spit.

Dead level they sped into the final stretch. Spit's slight figure was poised fearlessly on his trolley, drawing the extremes of speed from her. Thundering beside him, anxious but determined, came Leslie. He was actually drawing ahead – and forcing his way to the top of the camber. On they came like two charioteers – Spit delicately edging to the side, to gain inches by the extra downward momentum. I kept my eyes fastened clean across the road as they came belting past the winning-post.

First past was the plate *The British Queen*. I saw that first. Then I saw the heavy rear wheel jog over a pothole and strike Spit's front wheel – sending him in a swerve across the road. Suddenly then, from nowhere, a charabanc came speeding round the wide bend.

Spit was straight in its path. Nothing could avoid the collision. I gave a cry of fear as I saw the heavy solid tyre of the front wheel hit the trolley. Spit was flung up and his back hit the radiator. Then the driver stopped dead.

I got there first. Spit was lying on the macadam road on his side. His face was white and dusty, and coming out between his lips and trickling down his chin was a rivulet of fresh red blood.

Scattered all about him were yellow rose petals.

'Not my fault,' I heard the driver shouting. 'I didn't have a chance. He came straight at me.'

The next thing we were surrounded by women who had got out of the charabanc. And then Leslie and all the lads came up.

'Somebody send for an ambulance!' called a woman.

'I'll run an' tell the gatekeeper to telephone,' said Ernie Haddock.

'I hadn't a chance,' the driver explained to the women.

'A piece of his jersey on the starting-handle there . . .' said someone.

'Don't move him,' said the driver to a stout woman who had bent over Spit. 'Wait for the ambulance.'

'Hush up,' she said. She knelt and put a silk scarf under Spit's head. Then she wiped his mouth with her little handkerchief.

He opened his eyes. Glazed they were, as though he couldn't see. A short cough came out of him, then he looked at me and his lips moved.

'*Who won?*'

'Thee!' blurted out Leslie. 'Tha just licked me. Eh, Bill?'

'Aye,' I said, 'old *Egdam* just pipped *The British Queen*.'

Spit's eyes closed again. The women looked at each other. They nearly all had tears in their eyes. Then Spit looked up again, and his wise, knowing look came over his face. After a minute he spoke in a sharp whisper:

'Liars. I can remember seeing Leslie's back wheel hit my front 'un. I didn't win – I lost.' He stared upward for a few seconds, then his eyes twitched and shut.

The driver kept repeating how it wasn't his fault, and next thing the ambulance came. Nearly all the women were crying now, and I saw the look that went between the two men who put Spit on a stretcher – but I couldn't believe he was dead. I had to go into the ambulance with the attendant to give him particulars. I went up the step and sat down inside and looked out the little window as the driver slammed the doors. I saw the driver holding Leslie as a witness. Chick Dale was lifting the smashed-up *Egdam* on to the body of *The British Queen*. People with bunches of flowers in their hands stared after us as we drove off. Then I heard the ambulance man asking me Spit's name. Then he touched me on the elbow with his pencil and said:

'Where *did* he live?'

The Goalkeeper's Revenge and Other Stories **Bill Naughton**

I knew then. That word 'did' struck right into me. But for a minute I couldn't answer. I had to think hard, for the way he said it made it suddenly seem as though Spit Nolan had been dead and gone for ages.

The Old Allon   The old Allon was no speedster: I should think it might have done forty when in perfect tune. Since it was decarbonized once a week, it was often in perfect tune. Perfect for its age, that is. But if I could not hope successfully to challenge one and all to straight-and-level combat, I soon discovered that I could persuade the old machine to move about on rough stuff just about as nimbly as much newer and faster ones. Provided the gradient was not too severe, the old Allon could be, and was, coaxed along every cart track, muddy by-way, and slippery or rocky track, for miles around.

This discovery led to the formation of a loose confederacy of young motor-cyclists living in the district. We used to stage 'trials', with no cash, no prizes, and no bull: and I did better than I deserved merely because mine was by so wide a margin the most antiquated old crock competing that I rode it with more abandon than my pals. There was little you could do to the Allon to make it more battered and dejected-looking than it already was. This proved a towering advantage, for most of my friends owned pretty machines which they were naturally reluctant to ruin.

Such treatment as was meted out to the Allon spelled ruin to any piece of machinery, and the day came when it was stripped and rebuilt for the last time. On this occasion Hardy and I made a real job of it. The Allon had done all that could be expected of it in 'trials' – including rolling over and over down several steep hills, sometimes with its rider, sometimes without. Now, for its final fling, it was to be converted into a racer.

We were possibly influenced in our decision to strip and lighten the bike by the fact that most of its exterior fittings had already fallen off. At any rate, when we had finished our 'conversion', the Allon broke at least six laws, and Hardy's not having a licence made it seven on the day. It had no mudguards, no silencer, no licence, no horn, no lamps, and virtually no brakes. Certainly no brakes that the law would recognize as brakes. For the sake of lightness we had discarded the original brake fittings. All that remained was a length of steel rod resting loosely on one foot-rest, to apply the brake, the rider had to grope down until he found this rod, then heave like hell.

By one of the crudest and most revolting 'milling' operations in the whole history of engineering, we had reduced the weight of the flywheel to such an extent that the engine would not run at all on less than about half-throttle. We had advanced the

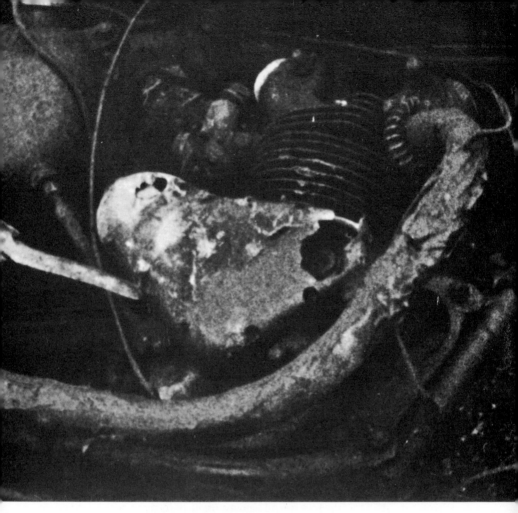

ignition timing as far as it would go and then a bit farther. We
had polished the piston head, the inlet port and the exhaust
port until they shone like silver. A short, straight-through
exhaust pipe emitted a shriek fit to wake the dead. Since the
decompressor valve in the cylinder head leaked, we had welded
it in position, permanently closed.

We scrapped the old-fashioned throttle levers and manufactured a highly unreliable twist-grip control, on the lines of
the racing grips which were just coming into vogue among the
top men, and which had the vice of repeatedly jamming the
bowden cable at the nipple and leaving the engine to race its
heart out, uncontrollably, on full bore. After one or two nasty
experiences with this we had become fairly adept at snatching

the lead off the sparking plug. Hardy was several times highly electrocuted while practising this manoeuvre. He said it made him feel fine.

The rebuild completed, we took the Allon on the road for the last time one grey Wednesday afternoon when we should have been playing compulsory football. In its highly modified form it was practically impossible to start, but once started, even more difficult to stop. The drill was that Hardy should push me on the old Allon down Broad Lane until I got the engine going, then nip back and get on the Coventry Eagle and catch me up. The Coventry Eagle was a smart little machine with a twin-port engine and the most fetching nickel-plated exhaust system in Bloxwich. There was no doubt in our minds that Hardy would be on my tail in a matter of minutes.

In fact, it worked out differently. We had to push the old Allon practically as far as Broad Lane Bridge before the darned thing would fire, and Hardy had nearly a quarter of a mile to run back to pick up the other machine. Once I was under power on the Allon, I knew that I should not see Hardy again that afternoon; if, indeed, ever.

It was a revelation. As if the poor old thing knew that this was its final outing, it put up the performance of its life. The ancient beast, stripped to a skeleton and turned out of all recognition, went howling down Broad Lane at a speed which I am prepared, with very little prodding, to put as high as fifty miles an hour. And that is a very solemn thought indeed. We leaped over the sharp crest of the canal bridge and came down into a snaking wobble which persisted for some two hundred yards, a fearful sinuous oscillation, about which I could do nothing, and than which I have experienced but few things nastier, and those all due to women.

By the grace of God it settled again on to a straight course, and we went tearing towards the level crossing. This was a very minor affair, used only by infrequent colliery trains shuffling across, on a side line, to load up at the Holly Bank pits. There was no bar, no gate. When a train was about to cross, a man simply stood in the middle of the road and signalled to road users, if any, that it would be just as well to tarry awhile. And he would chat amiably with tarriers about any of the innumerable matters which occupy the minds of reasonable men who have time to stand and stare. A pleasant sort of crossing.

I observed, with a trace of annoyance, that a train of coal

waggons was approaching, and the signalman was standing in the middle of the road waving me to a halt. Obediently, though with a touch of choler rising, I twisted the twist-grip to cut the engine. Nothing happened. The nipple had jammed again. The Allon and I went howling and screaming towards our doom. Lying flat on the tank, I groped for the ignition lead. I happened to touch the sparking plug instead. Several millions of volts animated my frame. I gave a convulsive wiggle, not surprising in the circumstances, and the old Allon went into a sympathetic wiggle of its own. Desperately I hauled on the brake rod, but even when I had got a grip on it, it had no effect save to make our wiggle more pronounced.

The crossing suddenly began to diminish as the train chugged over. The engine let out a great blast on its whistle. The signal-man leaped into the ditch. Wiggling like a samba dancer, shrieking like a space ship, the Allon and I leaped over the last available yard of level crossing. I felt the hot breath of the engine as we passed.

Faster and faster now we streaked towards Essington. A long straight lay ahead, very slightly downhill, and here we touched, I make bold to say, the highest speed ever reached by a 1921 two-stroke in private hands. I would not care to put a figure to it, but it was impressive. Fortunately the wiggle had once more ironed itself out, we were more or less straight-and-level, and there was nobody in sight. But I was just that little bit exercised in my mind because at the end of the long straight there was the choice, not to be dodged, of an acute turn to the left or a somewhat gentler, though still sharp, bend to the right. A sort of malformed T-junction. I made up my mind to try to take the right-hand turn, and prayed to God, with a happy innocence all things considered, that He would give me strength and skill to round that bend in one piece.

For there was no checking the old Allon. After experiencing the treatment once, I did not share Hardy's partiality for shock therapy. And I had discovered that hauling on the brake rod made not a blind bit of difference. It became clear to my far from nimble brain that I was faced with a choice between three alternatives. To throw myself off: unthinkable. To ride it straight into a hedge: possible, even probable. To press on regardless until the petrol supply gave out: dire, but somehow the most interesting alternative of the lot. So we approached the sharp right-hand bend, an interesting mixture of elation, remorse, and prayer.

Maurice Wiggin

**The Last
Great Tram Race**

Saturdays we went to the tram races were the most exciting days I knew. There were all the usual Saturday pleasures, but enhanced and drawn out by anticipation – the day-time fire in the sitting-room, newly lit as I got home from school soon after twelve, the sticks still crackling and the sharp smell as the coal started to bite; the wireless that was normally switched on only in the evening playing the special cheerful Saturday morning music that a kindly B.B.C. dispensed.

At lunch, which would always be cold ham, my father would drink a bottle of Worthington to mark the arrival of the weekend. The afternoon dragged by, with an expedition to buy sweets, then tea, with a poached egg on toast for my father and me because we would miss supper.

Finally we would set off in my father's Wolseley Hornet with my mother's anxious injunctions to us both to keep warm still ringing in my ears. The Mersey Tunnel had just been opened and going through it was very much of a part of the splendour of the occasion, even though on a Saturday evening in those days it would be almost empty; certainly there was little chance of meeting one of the J. V. Rank steam lorries with its firetray glowing red beneath the great high cab.

As we emerged from the Docks Exit it would be quite dark. The cobbled streets were badly lit, the brightest patches spilling from the open doors of the pubs and fish-and-chip shops.

The race-track, or Tramadome as they tried to call it – I never heard anyone use the name – was just off the main Southport road. The signs that we were nearing it always filled me with fresh excitement: the ordinary street trams that we encountered displaying their pink placards, TO & FROM THE TRAM RACES: the newspaper bills for the *Echo* and *Evening Express* and *Sunday Despatch*: the cloth-capped, mackintoshed pedestrians we would begin to overtake, at first in ones or twos, gradually coalescing into a procession as the rusty corrugated iron fence and ellipse of high overhead lights of the stadium beckoned.

The track at Liverpool was shaped rather like the railway track one might construct from a cheap model train set. Two short straights were joined by two curves, one appreciably wider than the other.

The trams would be standing like great stranded whales under the arc lights, mechanics and engineers working on them. Nearby the crews would be strutting around rather self-consciously in their racing overalls, sometimes drinking tea from enamel mugs or Guinness straight from the pint bottle, sometimes signing autographs for the fans who penetrated the paddock area. Strictly speaking it wasn't allowed but there always seemed to be a few there. I never tried myself, partly from timidity, partly because I knew my father would dis-approve, partly because I suspected that too close an acquaintance with the heroes whose names and exploits I knew by heart would be disheartening.

Next to the preparations I liked the start, which was always a moment of unalloyed excitement. The four trams in each heat would be lined up in echelon, like runners in the 220 yards, and as the one-minute bell went they would move forward keeping station. Down the back straight they would begin to gather speed until coming out of the south curve they would be doing perhaps 20 m.p.h. As the black marker cleared the points which followed the curve, the starter's flag would fall and with a final surge of power the four tall ships would leap forward while the crowd which had been holding its breath roared.

For the vehicle on the outside lane it meant almost immediate braking again for the north curve, a disadvantage which outweighed the higher cornering speed made possible by the wider radius. At Liverpool the middle two tracks were generally held to be the most favoured, but a really great driver like Keating or my particular hero, Gus Field from Meadowbank, Edinburgh, could triumph from any position.

Suddenly the gas organ ceased its tune and the distorted loudspeaker voice of the track announcer was giving the draw for places. I'd been craning over from my usual corner vantage point, watching my hero. He was leaning nonchalantly against the flank of his tram, smoking a Gold Flake and reading a paper. When we'd heard that he'd drawn the outside track – and a triumphant jeer from the crowd – he merely shrugged and ground the cigarette under his heel.

As the two-minute bell rang out the four vehicles took up their stations. Keating had his usual Birkenhead car, Robinson his Liverpool model. Field's mount was a Sheffield tram dating from the days when the more powerful cars from hilly cities had been fleetest – with the practice of re-winding and in some cases replacing the motors this generalization no longer applied. Steele had a great brute of a thing from Stockport.

He was drawn in the Number Two lane next to Field and towards the end of the rolling lap before the start it was quite obvious that he was creeping ahead of his proper station; so much so that as the flag fell he was almost level with Field's rear platform, Dobbie staring at him in blank astonishment.

Why the stewards didn't call for a restart was never properly explained. Perhaps they dared do nothing that might further inflame the crowd.

Anyway as the cars slammed into the first curve Field and Steele were neck and neck.

I shall never forget that race – the four trams seemingly locked together. Iron clashing and shrieking against iron, the drivers crouched over their controls, the conductors bracing themselves out from their platforms in an effort to add a last tiny ounce of stability, the sparks burning from the trolley-poles, the air full of the ozone-smell that was uniquely tram-racing's, the now-hushed crowd. . . .

Halfway through the third and last lap and Field had crept inexorably into the lead. Never had he driven so brilliantly, so disdainfully. He was going to win and Heaven knew what the crowd would say.

At this moment – disaster! He lost his overhead contact. Luckily he was already slowing down for the last bend and didn't lose speed – indeed, with the magnetic brake failing he entered the curve faster than ever before. If Dobbie could reconnect the trolley-pole quickly enough he could still hold off the others, and Dobbie, leaning dizzily out from his platform, hadn't become Field's partner for nothing. He had the current flowing again almost before the crowd had uttered its deep 'aaaah' that always greeted bad luck, on whomever it fell.

But then the murmur changed to a sound of shock and horror. For Steele, disregarding the unwritten law among tram-men, had not respected Dobbie's exposed position. Without even ringing his bell as a warning he forced his way up on the adjoining track. His superstructure caught the luckless Dobbie and sent him spinning into the corner of his platform with a terrible thud.

As his conductor was still officially aboard there was nothing to stop Field continuing the last hundred yards to victory. But he'd been darting rearward glances all the while and saw what had happened. Without hesitating he locked on every brake, brought his tram to a shuddering halt and without paying any more attention to the race ran back through the car to the aid of his partner.

Philip Purser

Poor Dobbie had a broken pelvis, a smashed arm, a hideously fractured leg. The crowd poured away curiously abashed. There had been worse accidents in the past, but this one seemed to have been the natural consequence of their own mood. My father hurried me home, and I never went tram-racing again.

The First Railway Engines and a Most Curious Optical Illusion

In the rapid movement of these engines, there is an optical deception worth mentioning. A spectator observing their approach, when at extreme speed, can scarcely divest himself of the idea, that they are not enlarging and increasing in size rather than moving. . . . At first the image is barely discernible, but as it advances from the focal point, it seems to increase beyond all limit. Thus an engine, as it draws near, appears to become rapidly magnified, and as if it would fill up the entire space between the banks, and absorb everything within its vortex.

Edward Stanley

The Makers of Speed

The silent litany of the workmen goes on –
Speed, speed, we are the makers of speed.
We make the flying, crying motors,
Clutches, brakes and axles,
Gears, ignitions, accelerators,
Spokes and springs and shock absorbers,
The silent litany of the workmen goes on –
Speed, speed, we are the makers of speed;
Axles, clutches, levers, shovels,
We make the signals and lay the way –
    Speed, speed.

The trees come down to our tools,
We carve the wood to the wanted shape.
The whining propeller's song in the sky,
The steady drone of the overland truck,
Comes from our hands; us; the makers of speed.

Speed; the turbines crossing the Big Pond,
Every nut and bolt, every bar and screw,
Every fitted and whirling shaft,
They come from us, the makers,
Us, who know how,
Us, the high designers and the automatic feeders,
Us, with heads,
Us, with hands,
Us, on the long haul, the short flight,
We are the makers, lay the blame on us –
Carl Sandburg   The makers of speed.

```
        I AM BARD
      I AM ISOBAR
    I AM IRON BAR
   I AM IRON BARD
   I AM BY ASGARD
 I AM IRON ICEBERG  great western suspension steam telegraph
     I STAND GUARD  great eastern hungerford canal cableboat
     I SPAN BARRED  great clifton railtunnel docks submarine
      I SEEM BARED  great britain explosions locks towerpier
       I STAB HARD
```

Construction for
Isambard Kingdom
Brunel
Edwin Morgan

BRUMEL
BOOMMILL
BROODWELL
BREWMETAL
BROOKMEDDLE
BRUNELLESCHAL
BLOOMMIDDLE
BLUEMEZZO
BOONMEDAL
BRUMMELL

The Little Giant   Much of the basic invention had been done when Victoria came to the throne. There was already, so to speak, a certain head of steam. Its power was beginning to be felt. It was a challenge eagerly seized by young men. It was a young man's world. Steam soon had its heroes. They lived in the sort of limelight enjoyed in our times, but more briefly, by film stars, athletes and, sometimes, five-star generals. They were not initiators, not necessarily the inventors of the engines which revolutionized time, space and industry. Their talents lay in the application and promotion of steam. They were practical dreamers, creative technicians, bold and versatile men of vision. . . . There was nothing they could not make steam do. At least, there was nothing they would not try to make it do. Their successes were glorious; so were some of their failures. As professionals, many of them were willing to concede that they had over-reached themselves but few were daunted by this, buoyed up as they may have been by an heroic sense that they were in fact living ahead of their times.

Foremost among such heroes was Isambard Kingdom Brunel who, with Daniel Gooch, drove the locomotive of the train bearing Queen Victoria from Slough to Paddington in 1842. This man, internationally known as the 'Little Giant', was already famous at the age of twenty, when he built the first tunnel shaft to be driven beneath a river; and himself came near to perishing in the waters of the Thames in achieving this. He built the Great Western Railway from London to Bristol. When he was thirty-two he built and launched the Great Western, the first steamship designed for ocean crossings. At thirty-seven he launched the Great Britain, the first iron-built ocean ship and the first to be driven entirely by a propeller. (Her hulk still lies in the Falkland Islands.) Brunel's vast invention and capacity are summarized by James Dugan in *The Great Iron Ship*:

The Little Giant built twenty-five railways in England, Ireland, Italy and India, and the precipitous Taff Vale line in Wales, considered a choice collectors' item by contemporary rail fans. He built eight piers and dry-docks, five suspension bridges, and 125 railway bridges. He invented the compartmented freight car, an innovation re-innovated a century later by U.S. railways. He introduced railway telegraphy in 1839. In 1825 he published an argument for a canal through the Isthmus of Panama. During the Crimean war he designed an armoured gunboat which would launch amphibious tanks to attack the Russian forts at Kronstadt. The vehicles were to be powered by jet propulsion. The idea was ninety years too early for the Admiralty. The War Office, however, carried out another Brunel design, a 1,500-bed military hospital, prefabricated in England (no part was too heavy for two men to carry) and erected at Renkioi, Turkey, by eighteen men in ten weeks. The hospital had excellent plumbing, and pumped 1,390 cubic feet of cooled humidified air per minute around each bed. While he was building the Great Eastern, Brunel was also managing the big railway hotel at Paddington Station, 'a very agreeable relaxation from his more important duties', said his son.

Some idea of the public esteem enjoyed by Brunel, even when he was still the young father of a family, can be drawn from a domestic accident which aroused the concern and interest of the whole nation. He swallowed a gold half-sovereign piece. He was performing one of his favourite parlour tricks in front of his assembled family. The half-sovereign had to pass from his ear to his mouth. It ended up in his right bronchus. When he jerked his head he felt the coin drop towards his glottis. He suffered paroxysms of coughing but had the presence of mind to call in his brother-in-law, Sir Benjamin Brodie, a leading surgeon, to tell him exactly where the coin was and how to reach it. This neither Brodie nor a panel of friends and medical experts which soon assembled could even begin to achieve.

Brunel characteristically took matters into his own hands. Invention was called for: and was he not one of the most ingenious men of his age? News of his misfortune was widely reported in the Press. London, and indeed the nation, was soon agog to learn that the Little Giant had designed a frame for himself – and it was an enviable feature of those times, that action and construction instantly followed a flight of thought. His was a pivoted contraption not unlike a dressmaker's swing mirror. Upon this he had himself strapped, then turned upside down. In that position he coughed and choked and was continually slapped on the back in the hope that this convulsive torture would eject the coin. Daily bulletins accompanied this treatment, which went on for weeks and was only halted when the medical men insisted that he was in danger of killing himself. They suggested a tracheotomy to which Brunel agreed, but not till he had designed special forceps for the job.

Without the use of any anaesthetic, Brodie made the throat incision. He then used the instrument (still known as Brodie's forceps) but he failed to reach the coin. Another attempt was made on the following day, without success. Then Brunel himself took the initiative again. On the third day, with the wound still open, he had himself once more strapped upside down to the coughing machine. After a short convulsion the coin fell back into his mouth.

The Golden Age of Steam
John Pudney

O Pioneers!   This Tunnel was bugn begubnugn in 1880 *Willliam Sharp*
[Workman's inscription on entrance to abandoned Channel Tunnel at Dover]

Channel Tunnel bugn.
1880. Sharp Wilgn.

Tannel Chunnel begum.
8018. Shart Willum.

Tennal Chennul gbung.
8081. Shant Willung.

Chennul Tennal bengug.
8108. Shunt Willibug.

Chunnal Tennel begbugn.
8801. Slunt Willubugmn.

Chuntenlannel begubnugn.
8810. Blunt Wuglbumlugn.

      *   *   *   *   *

Edwin Morgan   10880. Brigde bugn.

Coal-Mine

You start off, stooping slightly, down the dim-lit gallery, eight or ten feet wide and about five high, with the walls built up with slabs of shale, like the stone walls in Derbyshire. Every yard or two there are wooden props holding up the beams and girders; some of the girders have buckled into fantastic curves under which you have to duck. Usually it is bad going underfoot – thick dust or jagged chunks of shale, and in some places where there is water it is mucky as a farmyard. Also there is the track for the coal tubs, like a miniature railway track with sleepers a foot or two apart, which is tiresome to walk on. Everything is grey with shale dust; there is a dusty fiery smell which seems to be the same in all mines. You see mysterious machines of which you never learn the purpose, and bundles of tools slung together on wires, and sometimes mice darting away from the beam of the lamps. They are surprisingly common, especially in mines where there are or have been horses. It would be interesting to know how they got there in the first place; possibly by falling down the shaft – for they say a mouse can fall any distance un-injured, owing to its surface area being so large relative to its weight. You press yourself against the wall to make way for lines of tubs jolting slowly towards the shaft, drawn by an endless steel cable operated from the surface. You creep through sacking curtains and thick wooden doors which, when they are opened, let out fierce blasts of air. These doors are an important part of the ventilation system. The exhausted air is sucked out of one shaft by means of fans, and the fresh air enters the other of its own accord. But if left to itself the air will take the shortest way round, leaving the deeper workings unventilated; so all short cuts have to be partitioned off.

The Road to Wigan Pier
George Orwell

Mining Rhyming

Song-making proliferated among miners during the latter half of the nineteenth century. Looking back to his boyhood, an ex-collier from West Stanley, eighty years old when he was recorded in 1952, remarked: 'Making rhymes and songs used to run through the pit like a fever. Some of 'em seemed to go daft thinking up verses. Even us young lads used to answer back in rhyme. The men would get down, take a little walk, see what the last shift had done. The man who'd been working in your place had always left his smell behind him, and we'd even make a rhyme on that. One would say: "Whe's bin hewin in maa place in the oors since Aa've bin gan? Aa reckon it wes aad Basher wi's lavender hair-oil on." And another would answer: "Whe's bin hewin in maa place? Aa reckon it wes aad Rab. He's the only man in Joycey's eats onions wi his snap."'

food   A. J. Lloyd

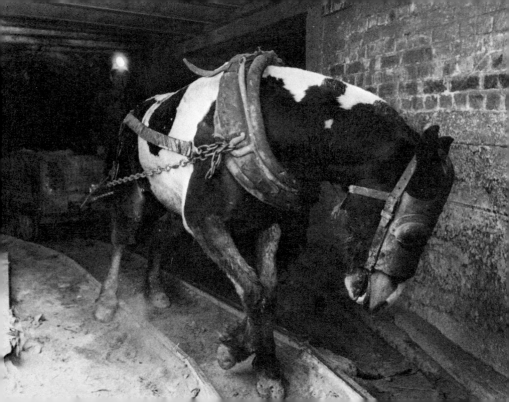

Out of the dirt and dark- ness I was born — Go down. Out of the hard, black coal face I was torn — Go down. Kicked on the world and the earth split o- pen, Crawled through a crack where the rock was bro- ken, Bur-rowed a hole a- way in the coal — Go down.

The Ballad of the Big Hewer

Out of the dirt and darkness I was born –
Go down.
Out of the hard, black coal face I was torn –
Go down.
Kicked on the world and the earth split open,
Crawled through a crack where the rock was broken,
Burrowed a hole away in the coal –
Go down.

In a cradle of coal in the darkness I was laid –
Go down.
Down in the dirt and darkness I was raised –
Go down.
Cut me teeth on a five foot timber,
Held up the roof with me little finger,
Started me time away in the mine –
Go down.

On the day that I was born I was six foot tall –
Go down.
And the very next day I learned the way to haul –
Go down,
And the third day worked at board and pillar,
Worked on the fourth as a long-wall filler,
Getting me steam up, hewing the seam –
Go down.

I'm the son of the son of the son of a collier's son –
Go down.
Coal dust flows in the veins where the blood should run –
Go down.
Five steel ribs and an iron backbone,
Teeth that can bite through rock and blackstone,
Working me time away in the mine –
Go down.

Three hundred years I hewed at the coal by hand –
Go down.
In the pits of Durham and East Northumberland –
Go down.
Been gassed and burned and blown asunder,
Buried more times than I can number,
Getting the coal, away in the hole –
Go down.

I've scrabbled and picked at the face where the roof was low –
Go down.
Crawled in the seams where only a mole could go –
Go down.
cleared   In the thin cut seams I've ripped and redded,
Where even the rats are born bow-legged,
Winning the coal away in the hole –
Go down.

I've worked in the Hutton, the Plessy, the Brockwell
   seam –
Go down.
The Bensham, the Busty, the Beaumont, the Marshall Green –
Go down.
I've lain on me back in the old three quarter,
Up to the chin in stinking water,
Hewing the coal away in the hole –
Go down.

Out of the dirt and darkness I was born –
Go down.
Out of the hard black coal face I was torn –
Go down.
Lived in the shade of the high pit heap,
Am still down there where the seams are deep,
But digging the coal away in the hole –
Ewan MacColl   Go down.

77

from **The Ballad of the Big Hewer**

'When you hew a lump of coal, you know that you are the only one that has seen it. You are the first one to see it.'

'Oh dear, a complete new world, strange world entirely. Although it was well-lit. Electric light at the pit bottom. But once we turned our backs on the pit bottom and going into narrow places and down into the darkness, then the experience was so horrible and terrible. I was frightened now, I didn't know where I was going.'

'The silence in the pit, it's, it's like infinity or the bottom of the ocean. It's, it's peaceful and yet it's sometimes frightening. You could be driven to panic with it I think. You've never known absolute blackness, always the stars at night, and there's always the moon. But there, there's nothing, and you can feel this pressing on you, the darkness, you can *feel* this darkness.'

'I think if I cut my fingers and it bled, it would just come out black.'

'You're not working with a piece of land, you're working with the world.'

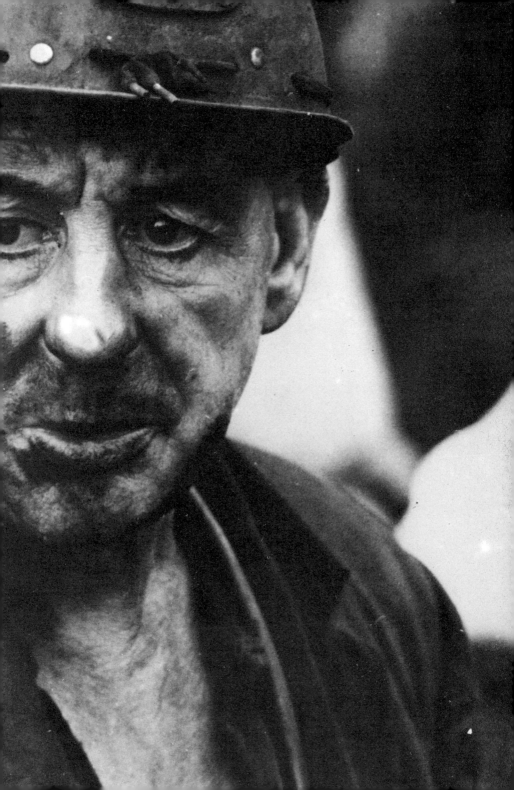

'All they had was their pride, and oftentimes when there was
the greatest need there was the greatest pride. And an
unwillingness to go and seek assistance of any kind. The miner
has always had the pride thing. He thinks, well, if he can't
make his living by the muscles of his hands and his legs, well,
he just doesn't want it.'

'An old mate of mine, Dai Mardeer they called him, was
driving a big horse in a low seam, in a low level. So when the
fireman came around the top was very very hard and the
fireman said, "Well, what you want to do is to cut a bit from
under his feet so that the horse would go lower." So Dai
looked at him and muttered something under his breath and
the fireman went on his way. He came past that way about an
hour later and he saw Dai banging like blazes at the top. He
said, "What on earth are you doing there, Dai? I told you to
cut a bit under his feet." He said, "Look, mate, you can't kid
me," he said, "It's his ears are catching, not his feet."'

When Isaac Lewis passed away,
What do you think they done,
Sold him off for anthracite,
At £20 a ton.

'He had a good remedy for hard roof. He told the manager he
had a remedy, "Leave the coal under it." '

'Coal's a thing that costs life to get. You may be holding a
piece of coal in your hand and turn round and say, "I wonder
how that coal was got? Was there any blood shed near that
coal? Was any man's life lost in it?" And there's many a one in
this country has put coal on the fire and there's been a man's
life lost on it. You're not burning coal, you're burning blood.'

'To compare the old days to the present day working – like
changing two worlds; or if you'd like to compare a miner, I say
in the old days he was a mole groping in the dark and
burrowing in complete darkness. But today, in comparison,
he's like a peacock able to see almost next to daylight. And he is
very proud of himself – as proud as that peacock.'

'Deep down in a man's heart, he feels he loves it. He loves
the earth. Everything that you use in this world comes from
the earth. Your own self comes from the earth, the water you
drink comes from the earth, the food you eat, in some shape
or form, the tools you use, the wood you use, the match you
use, the chairs you sit on. They all come from the earth. When
you die you go back there.'

Anonymous

News MARY There's somebody at the door.

THOMAS You're hearing things, woman.

MARY I'm telling you there is. . . .

   [*And there is. And a slow realization of what it might mean*]

MARY I'll go.

   [*Mary goes to the door. She greets Hughie – the pit messenger*]

HUGHIE Mrs Milburn.

MARY You know it is. . . .

HUGHIE Your grandson John works at the pit. . . .

MARY I know he does. . . .

HUGHIE There's been an accident.

RUTH No. . . .

THOMAS Quiet!

MARY What sort of accident?

HUGHIE A fall of stone . . . John was working with his maintenance gang . . . on the face . . . we don't know exactly where they are . . . just the other side . . . no contact, you see. . . .

[Silent reactions]

As soon as there's any more news.

MARY Yes.

HUGHIE Other calls to make.

Alan Plater   MARY Yes.

Pig at Machine   Directly in front of me was the biggest machine I had ever seen. I judged from the noise it made and from the great stream of white sparks that hosed out from one side of it that it was a surface-grinder, but what a surface-grinder. You could have ground the walls of a house on it. The grinding wheel, which I calculated must have been as big as a large cartwheel, was completely hidden from view under a metal cowl that was the shape and size of a small oasthouse, the inside of which became by turns as bright as looking at the sun and black as midnight. . . .

I started to walk round the machine, and was accompanied all down one side by the table, moving only slightly faster than I walked. By the time I had walked across the end, however, it was under the cowl again, flashing and crashing like a great rocket straining to take off. I tried to keep my eyes away from it, but the cowl was now in front of me. When the last casting had gone through and my eyes had cleared, I was standing at the base of the cowl, and found myself looking at a formidable control panel with coloured lights, and a large, scaly pig. The pig glanced at me briefly and continued winding a wheel. The wheel had a handle on it, but the pig wound it by putting its nose between two of the four spokes of the wheel and twiddling expertly and very quickly. The pig brought the wheel to a halt, gave it a last nudge or two, withdrew its nose and glanced up at the dials and lights. Evidently satisfied, it took a short, knobbed lever carefully in its mouth and pushed it to the right. I perceived that the table was now returning. The pig ambled off past me with a sniff and a snort. I caught sight of the operator of the next machine along, who was human and looking in my direction, so I waved and walked towards him. I was met halfway by the great table, its cargo of castings, smoking slightly and glinting from ground surfaces as it passed me.

As I approached the next machine I saw that this was a powerful press, such as is used to punch or press out shapes from flat plates of soft steel. Its heavy bedplate, cut across with deep grooves for clamping, was straddled by four shining steel pillars as thick as a man's thigh, which supported the great ram, together with a flywheel like a millstone and various devices for starting and stopping the ram. Clamped to the bedplate was the large piece of metal which forms what is in effect the teeth of the press, if the bed may be looked on as the lower jaw and the ram as the upper. The raw material was being fed through this now, and every few seconds there

was a loud click and the ram dropped as if struck from above by some gigantic hammer, and returned. Each time it did so the ground shook, but the machine was not as noisy as most. The man, who continued to work the machine and feed the metal through in a long strip, greeted me very cheerfully. . . .

'Good morning,' I said. 'I was very surprised to see a pig in charge of a surface-grinder.'

The man laughed, a great generous, bubbling laugh like a slap on the back.

'Yes, he's a pig all right! Look at him now.'

I looked. The pig was standing at a point beside the cowl where a shower of sparks was escaping, in such a position that most of them impinged on his back. They bounced off him in all directions, covering him from nose to tail in a shimmering umbrella. On his face was an expression which was very like a smile.

'He loves that,' said my comrade. 'Like having his back scratched, I suppose. That's why they gave him the job really, not because he's much of a pig.'

'Oh?' I said.

'No, I have to set up for him and put him right and so on. Mind you, he manages pretty well after that.'

Hanging on the wall between the two machines I saw a large notice covered in small type, headed 'Factories Act 1961 – Notes on the Employment of Pigs', beneath it in smaller type 'To be displayed in a prominent place wherever pigs are employed'. I walked over and looked at it. It was very long, but was divided into sections headed 'Safety', 'Health', 'Welfare', and 'Payment'. There was a paragraph on cleanliness, which stated that 'all accumulated dirt and refuse must be removed daily', and another which stipulated that every pig must have a minimum of 400 cu. ft. in which to work. There were paragraphs on temperature, ventilation, lighting, drainage of floors, 'Adequate Sanitary Accommodation' (which had to be separate for boars and sows) and facilities for sitting 'where sitting would not interfere with the work carried out'. Under 'Piecework Particulars' it said that every pig employed in piecework 'must have supplied to him such written particulars of the rates paid to him and the amounts of work done by him as to enable him to calculate the wage due to him'.

Peter C. Brown

Repairing a Joint   The pumps thrashed their quickening beat, and suddenly Thias stiffened. In the confusing blend of tremendous noise about him his ear had caught a new note – a hiss of steam that should not be there.

Darting inside he checked over the whole installation systematically, starting where the main steam-pipe came into the engine house from the boilers. The hissing noise could come from only one thing – escaping steam – and he had to locate the trouble quickly, and find out how serious it was.

There were three possibilities: a blown-out gland, a blown-out joint, or a broken pipe. If it was either of the first two he might be able to fix it right away by tightening down a couple of nuts: and even if this couldn't be done, the repair could wait till the heat was finished. But a broken pipe would be more serious, and a job for the mill-wrights which would mean shutting down the engine.

Quickly his eyes moved along the maze of pipes, pausing momentarily at each joint, and in less than a minute from first hearing the noise he found the trouble.

It was a blown joint on one of the smaller lines running to an auxiliary pump, and without wasting any more time he went to the store cupboard to collect the gear to repair it.

By the time the pumps slowed to a stop and Joe came in he had everything ready for the job – two three-quarter inch spanners for the nuts, a cold chisel, asbestos jointing, and graphite paste – and was shutting off the steam.

Joe saw the preparations and nodded his head approvingly.

'Joint gone?' he said in his funny terse way. 'Want me to help?' Thias grinned. 'I'd like to have a shot at it myself. I think I can manage.'

'Go ahead, son,' answered Joe. 'But mind you get the flanges clean and tighten up your nuts evenly.'

The first thing was to take the joint apart. Each section of pipe finished in a flat collar or flange, projecting at right angles to the run of the pipe. These flanges were pierced with holes for bolts, in this case seven three-quarter-inch bolts, which held the two pipe sections together. Between the flanges was put a piece of asbestos jointing, soft and resistant to heat, previously smeared with the graphite paste. When the nuts were tightened down the flanges bit into the graphite and asbestos, and made a joint through which the steam even at high pressure could not escape. In course of time the heat of the steam in the pipes would destroy the resisting qualities of the asbestos, and then the joint would blow and have to be remade. This had happened now.

Thias struck a snag right away. Six of the nuts loosened back after two or three hard blows with the hammer on the stem of the spanner. The seventh was not so easy. The nut slackened all right, then locked again, and the whole bolt began to turn. This was where the second spanner came in. Fixing it on the head of the bolt he turned until it was jammed in position against the pipe, then half a dozen taps with the hammer on the first spanner did the trick.

Thias took out the bolts and, bracing himself to take the weight of the pipes, allowed the two sections to come apart, then when he had scraped the faces of the flanges clean he turned to the jointing.

This came from the store in sheets about three feet square, and looked like a rather special kind of cardboard. The job was to cut from the sheet a disk exactly the size of the flange with a hole in the centre exactly the size of the inside of the pipe, and seven holes around the edge exactly the size of the bolt holes and in exactly the same position in relation to each other. Of course with a pair of compasses, a ruler and protractor, and a very sharp knife, it would be possible, but would take quite a long time. There was a simpler way, and a much surer and quicker one, that Joe had shown him.

Holding the sheet of jointing on the flange he took the hammer and, using the ball end of it, tapped lightly all round the inside edge of the pipe. The edge was sharp, and the hard metal cut easily through the soft asbestos, and in less than three minutes Thias had his centre hole. The rest was easy, for now he had a guide, and quickly he tapped out a disk against the outer edge of the flange, and then the seven bolt holes, each one in exactly the right position.

With the jointing ready and smeared on both sides with graphite, he wiped off the faces of the flanges, slipped it into place, and slid in the first bolt, flicking the nut on to hold it. Then, dipping the thread of each in oil to prevent corrosion, he put in the others and began tightening up. This was the most important part of the whole job, for a good joint depended on the two flanges being drawn together evenly. First of all he

tightened down each nut by hand, easing the pipe with his shoulder as he did so. Then, taking the spanner, he pulled on each in turn, until he could move them no further, and finally, with the hammer, drove them all up as far as they would go.

When he was satisfied he turned on the steam, and for a moment looked at what he had done. It was all right so far, but the test would be time, and every day that passed before that particular joint blew out again would be proof of his good workmanship.

He turned to gather up the tools, and only then did he remember the lost heat which had so absorbed him earlier in the day.

Jim had not turned up. He must have got hung up on some special job.

Sabotage at the Forge **Richard Armstrong**

Thias put the gear away, and, wiping his hands on a wad of cotton waste, picked up his oil cans and set out for the foreman's office.

Bench Dreams There are nine benches down the line, a man standing at each. We make all the tractor parts in our shop. On our line we panel-beat the hoods, each man doing his part of the work and then manhandling it on to the next man, and so on, until it gets to me. We do two hundred and sixty hoods a day, and it only takes me two minutes to do my bit of it, though I was timed for ten minutes by the time-study man. When there aren't enough hoods to make up our two hundred and sixty a day we 'borrow' from the next day – and then forget the next day that we borrowed them. . . . So there are nine men all told who work on our line, and each one is a character, an individual in his own right. My work comes to me in a completely automatic way, in the gestures of an automaton. With a rag wrapped round my eyes I could still do it, and could do dozens before I realized that I had done any at all. But underneath this my mind never stops working. It lives by itself. Some call it dreaming, and if so, I am dreaming all day long, five days a week.

The whole bench dreams like this. It is a galley of automatons locked in dreams. Someone who has something to say to you has to come right up to your ear and scream into it before you can wake up or answer. If you aren't working – or dreaming – in this way, you say you aren't in the swing of it, and you do less of your stint.

I dream I am a painter painting great big pictures full of vivid outlandish colours. One day last week I found myself dreaming I was a gravedigger, my mind turning up soil and roots while my body was panel-beating a hood. Some days I am a hired assassin, or settling all problems in some clockwork and dream-like revolution. Or I am writing a book about the dreams I am dreaming, or about factory thoughts running through my head if I am neither doing one thing nor the other. . . .

Bryan Slater If you didn't dream at work it would send you mad. It isn't the actual work that kills you in a factory. It's the *repetition*.

**Recitative for
Punished Products**

I was once a tire. To bolster sales
My cunning maker filled me full of nails.
My treads were shredded. I was made a flat
By great machines designed to do just that.

I was a typewriter. Harsh was my test.
Ten years I toiled unoiled without a rest.
One billion times, so claim the pedagogues,
The quick brown foxes jumped my lazy cogs.

I used to be a watch. My tick and tock
Were interchanged by polychronic shock.
The bit of bounce my spring retained was sapped
By tales of clocks alarmed, of watches strapped.

I am a shears. My thin lips prophesy
The Day to Come when angles cloud the sky,
When rugs rise up, mute tools get out of hand,
And crazed computers walk the frenzied land.

All:
Awesome the clangs will be, fearful the whirs
John Updike   When products punish manufacturers.

Found Poem

Dear Sir,

By the time I arrived at the house where you sent me to make
repairs, the storm had torn a good fifty bricks from the roof.
So I set up on the roof of the building a beam and a pulley and
I hoisted up a couple of baskets of bricks. When I had finished
repairing the building there were a lot of bricks left over since I
had brought up more than I needed and also because there
were some bad, reject bricks that I still had left to bring down.
I hoisted the basket back up again and hitched up the line at
the bottom. Then I climbed back up again and filled up the
basket with the extra bricks. Then I went down to the bottom
and untied the line. Unfortunately, the basket of bricks was
much heavier than I was and before I knew what was
happening, the basket started to plunge down, lifting me
suddenly off the ground. I decided to keep my grip and hang
on, realizing that to let go would end in disaster – but halfway
up I ran into the basket coming down and received a severe
blow on the shoulder. I then continued to the top, banging my
head against the beam and getting my fingers jammed in the
pulley. When the basket hit the ground it burst its bottom,
allowing all the bricks to spill out. Since I was now heavier than
the basket I started back down again at high speed. Halfway
down, I met the basket coming up, and received several severe
injuries on my shins. When I hit the ground, I landed on the
bricks, getting several more painful cuts and bruises from the
sharp edges.

Translated from the   At this moment I must have lost my presence of mind, because
French by   I let go of the line. The basket came down again, giving me
Michael Benedikt   another heavy blow on the head, and putting me in the hospital.
Jean L'Anselme   I respectfully request sick leave.

'*Don't keep saying thank you!*'

Frogman 1 Unsettling silt
In the holds of liners,

Nudging about
Under greasy piers, wrench,

File and crowbar
Remotely in contact,

Cantilevers
Coming and going on

The strength of bolts
He had better locate –

He bargained for
All that. It was a job.

2 Now after hours
  In the dirtiest reach

  He tries old tyres,
  Petrol drums, carcasses

  And pokes about
  In the slimiest clefts.

  His bubbling plume
  Surrenders to currents,

  No one watches
  Its sud on the surface.

3 He's slipped away
  Beyond blueprints and planned dives.

  When he rises
  There's no audience or foreman

  Owns or tells him.
  He's nobody's feeler

  For drownings or
  Sinkings or loose bridges.

  It's come to be
  He just loves the water.

4 The straitjacket
  Of clock and calendar

  Dissolves, the bed
  Of the river is soft –

  It's not overtime
  Keeps him here at all.

  The air's a slap
  In the face. He always

  Walks home late now
  In rubber and goggles.

Seamus Heaney

Doing Nothing We watched things: we watched people build houses, we watched men fix cars, we watched each other patch bicycle tires with rubber bands. We watched men dig ditches, climb telephone poles – I can hear the sound now of climbing irons on a pole, this was a race of heroes! – we watched trains at the station, shoe-shine men at the station, Italian men playing *boccie*, our fathers playing cards, our mothers making jam, our sisters skipping rope, curling their hair. For at least a month I watched my sisters making beads: they cut paper into long triangular strips, put glue on them, wrapped them around hatpins, and then I think they varnished them. I don't recall that they ever wore them, but I'm here to tell you they made them. They also did something called tie-dying: it was a rage, and it produced handkerchiefs of unbelievable ugliness.

bowls

We strung beads on strings: we strung spools on strings; we tied each other up with string, and belts and clothesline.

We sat in boxes; we sat under porches; we sat on roofs; we sat on limbs of trees.

We stood on boards over excavations; we stood on tops of piles of leaves; we stood under rain dripping from the eaves; we stood up to our ears in snow.

marbles We looked at things like knives and immies and pignuts and grasshoppers and clouds and dogs and people.

We skipped and hopped and jumped. Not going anywhere – just skipping and hopping and jumping and galloping.

We sang and whistled and hummed and screamed.

Robert Paul Smith What I mean, Jack, we did a lot of nothing.

Used Trout Stream On the other side of the Time filling station was the Cleveland Wrecking Yard. I walked down there to have a look at the used trout stream. The Cleveland Wrecking Yard has a very long front window filled with signs and merchandise.

There was a sign in the window advertising a laundry marking machine for $65.00. The original cost of the machine was $175.00. Quite a saving.

There was another sign advertising new and used two and three ton hoists. I wondered how many hoists it would take to move a trout stream.

There was another sign that said:

THE FAMILY GIFT CENTER
GIFT SUGGESTIONS FOR THE ENTIRE FAMILY

The window was filled with hundreds of items for the entire family. *Daddy, do you know what I want for Christmas? What son? A bathroom. Mommy, do you know what I want for Christmas? What Patricia? Some roofing materials.*

There were jungle hammocks in the window for distant relatives and dollar-ten-cent gallons of earth-brown enamel paint for other loved ones.

There was also a big sign that said:

USED TROUT STREAM FOR SALE
MUST BE SEEN TO BE APPRECIATED

I went inside and looked at some ship's lanterns that were for sale next to the door. Then a salesman came up to me and said in a pleasant voice, 'Can I help you?'

'Yes,' I said. 'I'm curious about the trout stream you have for sale. Can you tell me something about it? How are you selling it?'

'We're selling it by the foot length. You can buy as little as you want or you can buy all we've got left. A man came in here this morning and bought 563 feet. He's going to give it to his niece for a birthday present,' the salesman said.

'We're selling the waterfalls separately, of course, and the trees and birds, flowers, grass and ferns we're also selling extra. The insects we're giving away free with a minimum purchase of ten feet of stream.'

'How much are you selling the stream for?' I asked.

'Six dollars and fifty cents a foot,' he said. 'That's for the first hundred feet. After that it's five dollars a foot. . . .'

'What do the trout cost?' I asked.

'They come with the stream,' he said. 'Of course it's all luck. You never know how many you're going to get or how big they are. But the fishing's very good, you might say it's excellent. Both bait and dry fly,' he said smiling.

'Where's the stream at?' I asked. 'I'd like to take a look at it.'

'It's around in back,' he said. 'You go straight through that door and then turn right until you're outside. It's stacked in lengths. You can't miss it. The waterfalls are upstairs in the used plumbing department.'

'What about the animals?'

'Well, what's left of the animals are straight back from the stream. You'll see a bunch of our trucks parked on a road by the railroad tracks. Turn right on the road and follow it down past the piles of lumber. The animal shed's right at the end of the lot.'

'Thanks,' I said. 'I think I'll look at the waterfalls first. You don't have to come with me. Just tell me how to get there and I'll find my own way.'

'All right,' he said. 'Go up those stairs. You'll see a bunch of doors and windows, turn left and you'll find the used plumbing department. Here's my card if you need any help.'

'Okay,' I said. 'You've been a great help already. Thanks a lot. I'll take a look around.'

'Good luck,' he said.

I went upstairs and there were thousands of doors there. I'd never seen so many doors before in my life. You could have built an entire city out of those doors. Doorstown. And there were enough windows up there to build a little suburb entirely out of windows. Windowsville.

I turned left and went back and saw the faint glow of pearl-colored light. The light got stronger and stronger as I went further back, and then I was in the used plumbing department, surrounded by hundreds of toilets.

The toilets were stacked on shelves. They were stacked five toilets high. There was a skylight above the toilets that made them glow like the Great Taboo Pearl of the South Sea movies.

Stacked over against the wall were the waterfalls. There were about a dozen of them, ranging from a drop of a few feet to a drop of ten or fifteen feet.

There was one waterfall that was over sixty feet long. There were tags on the pieces of the big falls describing the correct order for putting the falls back together again.

The waterfalls all had price tags on them. They were more expensive than the stream. The waterfalls were selling for $19.00 a foot.

I went into another room where there were piles of sweet-smelling lumber, glowing a soft yellow from a different color skylight above the lumber. In the shadows at the edge of the room under the sloping roof of the building were many sinks and urinals covered with dust, and there was also another waterfall about seventeen feet long, lying there in two lengths and already beginning to gather dust.

I had seen all I wanted of the waterfalls, and now I was very curious about the trout stream, so I followed the salesman's directions and ended up outside the building.

O, I had never in my life seen anything like that trout stream. It was stacked in piles of various lengths: ten, fifteen, twenty feet, etc. There was one pile of hundred-foot lengths. There was also a box of scraps. The scraps were in odd sizes ranging from six inches to a couple of feet.

There was a loudspeaker on the side of the building and soft music was coming out. It was a cloudy day and seagulls were circling high overhead.

Behind the stream were big bundles of trees and bushes. They were covered with sheets of patched canvas. You could see the taps and roots sticking out the ends of the bundles.

crayfish

I went up close and looked at the lengths of stream. I could see some trout in them. I saw one good fish. I saw some crawdads crawling around the rocks at the bottom.

Richard Brautigan

It looked like a fine stream. I put my hand in the water. It was cold and felt good.

The Mechanical Hound The Mechanical Hound slept but did not sleep, lived but did not live in its gently humming, gently vibrating, softly illuminated kennel back in a dark corner of the firehouse. The dim light of one in the morning, the moonlight from the open sky framed through the great window, touched here and there on the brass and the copper and the steel of the faintly trembling beast. Light flickered on bits of ruby glass and on sensitive capillary hairs in the nylon-brushed nostrils of the creature that quivered gently, gently, gently, its eight legs spidered under it on rubber-padded paws.

Montag slid down the brass pole. He went out to look at the city and the clouds had cleared away completely, and he lit a cigarette and came back to bend down and look at the Hound. It was like a great bee come home from some field where the honey is full of poison wildness, of insanity and nightmare, its body crammed with that over-rich nectar and now it was sleeping the evil out of itself.

'Hello,' whispered Montag, fascinated as always with the dead beast, the living beast.

At night when things got dull, which was every night, the men slid down the brass poles, and set the ticking combinations of the olfactory system of the Hound and let loose rats in the firehouse area-way, and sometimes chickens, and sometimes cats that would have to be drowned anyway, and there would be betting to see which the Hound would seize first. The animals were turned loose. Three seconds later the game was done, the rat, cat, or chicken caught half across the area-way, gripped in gentling paws while a four-inch hollow steel needle plunged down from the proboscis of the Hound to inject massive jolts of morphine or procaine. The pawn was then tossed in the incinerator. The new game began.

Montag stayed upstairs most nights when this went on. There had been a time two years ago when he had bet with the best of them, and lost a week's salary and faced Mildred's insane anger, which showed itself in veins and blotches. But now at night he lay in his bunk, face turned to the wall, listening to whoops of laughter below and the piano-string scurry of rat feet, the violin squeaking of mice, and the great shadowing, motioned silence of the Hound leaping out like a moth in the raw light, finding, holding its victim, inserting the needle and going back to its kennel to die as if a switch had been turned.

Montag touched the muzzle.

The Hound growled.

Montag jumped back.

The Hound half rose in its kennel and looked at him with green-blue neon light flickering in its suddenly activated eye-bulbs. It growled again, a strange rasping combination of electrical sizzle, a frying sound, a scraping of metal, a turning of cogs that seemed rusty and ancient with suspicion.

'No, no, boy,' said Montag, his heart pounding.

He saw the silver needle extended upon the air an inch, pull back, extend, pull back. The growl simmered in the beast and it looked at him.

Montag backed up. The Hound took a step from its kennel. Montag grabbed the brass pole with one hand. The pole, reacting, slid upward, and took him through the ceiling, quietly. He stepped off in the half-lit deck of the upper level. He was trembling and his face was green-white. Below, the Hound had sunk back down upon its eight incredible insect legs and was humming to itself again, its multi-faceted eyes at peace.

Montag stood, letting the fears pass, by the drop-hole. Behind him, four men at a card table under a green-lidded light in the corner glanced briefly but said nothing. Only the man with the Captain's hat and the sign of the Phoenix on his hat, at last, curious, his playing cards in his thin hand, talked across the long room.

Fahrenheit 451
Ray Bradbury

'Montag . . . ?'

'It doesn't *like* me,' said Montag.

Life in the Machine   Imagine, if you can, a small room, hexagonal in shape, like the
cell of a bee. It is lighted neither by window nor lamp, yet it is
filled with a soft radiance. There are no apertures for ventilation, yet the air is fresh. There are no musical instruments,
and yet, at the moment that my meditation opens, this room is
throbbing with melodious sounds. An arm-chair is in the
centre, by its side a reading-desk – that is all the furniture. And
in the arm-chair there sits a swaddled lump of flesh – a woman,
about five feet high, with a face as white as a fungus. It is to her
that the little room belongs.

An electric bell rang.

The woman touched the switch and the music was silent.

'I suppose I must see who it is,' she thought, and set her chair
in motion. The chair, like the music, was worked by machinery,
and it rolled her to the other side of the room, where the bell
still rang importunately.

'Who is it?' she called. Her voice was irritable, for she had been
interrupted often since the music began. She knew several
thousand people; in certain directions human intercourse had
advanced enormously.

But when she listened into the receiver, her white face wrinkled
into smiles, and she said:

'Very well. Let us talk. I will isolate myself. I do not expect
anything important will happen for the next five minutes – for
I can give you fully five minutes, Kuno. Then I must deliver
my lecture on "Music during the Australian Period".'

She touched the isolation knob so that no one else could speak
to her. Then she touched the lighting apparatus and the little
room was plunged into darkness.

'Be quick!' she called, her irritation returning. 'Be quick,
Kuno; here I am in the dark wasting my time.'

But it was fully fifteen seconds before the round plate that she
held in her hands began to glow. A faint blue light shot across
it, darkening to purple, and presently she could see the image of
her son, who lived on the other side of the world, and he could
see her.

'Kuno, how slow you are.'

He smiled gravely.

'I really believe you enjoy dawdling.'

'I have called you before, mother, but you were always busy or isolated. I have something particular to say.'

'What is it, dearest boy? Be quick. Why should you not send it by pneumatic post?'

'Because I prefer saying such a thing. I want – '

'Well?'

'I want you to come and see me.'

Vashti watched his face in the pale blue plate.

'But I can see you!' she exclaimed. 'What more do you want?'

'I want to see you not through the Machine,' said Kuno. 'I want to speak to you not through the wearisome Machine.'

'Oh hush!' said his mother, vaguely shocked. 'You mustn't say anything against the Machine.'

'Why not?'

'One mustn't.'

'You talk as if a god had made the Machine,' cried the other. 'I believe that you pray to it when you are unhappy. Men made it, do not forget that. Great men, but men. The Machine is much, but it is not everything. I see something like you in this plate but I do not see you. I hear something like you through this telephone, but I do not hear you. That is why I want you to come. Come and stop with me. Pay me a visit, so that we can meet face to face, and talk about the hopes that are in my mind.'

She replied that she could scarcely spare the time for a visit.

'The airship barely takes two days to fly between me and you.'

'I dislike airships.'

'Why?'

The Machine Stops
E. M. Forster

'I dislike seeing the horrible brown earth, and the sea, and the stars when it is dark. I get no ideas in an airship.'

The Computer's Second Christmas Card

goodk kkkkk <u>unjam</u> ingwe nches lass? <u>start</u> <u>again</u> goodk

lassw enche skihg <u>start</u> <u>again</u> kings tart! <u>again</u> <u>sorry</u>

goodk ingwe ncesl ooked outas thef? <u>unmix</u> asloo kedou

tonth effff <u>rewri</u> tenow goodk ingwe ncesl asloo kedou

tonth effff fffff <u>unjam</u> feast ofsai ntste venst efanc

<u>utsai</u> <u>ntrew</u> <u>ritef</u> easto fstep toes<u>o</u> <u>rry</u>an dson<u>s</u> <u>orry</u>!

<u>start</u> <u>again</u> good? <u>y</u>esgo odkin gwenc eslas looke dout?

doubt <u>wrong</u> <u>track</u> <u>start</u> <u>again</u> goodk ingwe ncesl asloo

kedou tonth efeas tofst ephph phphp hphph <u>unjam</u> phphp

<u>repea</u> <u>tunja</u> <u>mhphp</u> <u>scrub</u> <u>carol</u> hphph <u>repea</u> <u>tscru</u> bcarc

<u>lstop</u> <u>subst</u> <u>itute</u> <u>track</u> merry chris tmasa ndgoo dnewy

earin 1699? <u>check</u> <u>digit</u> <u>banks</u> <u>orryi</u> n1966 <u>endme</u> <u>ssage</u>

Edwin Morgan

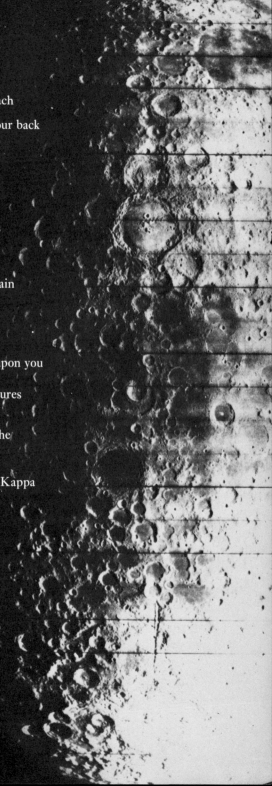

**After the Flight
of Ranger VII**

Moon
old fossil
to be scrubbed
and studied
like a turtle's stomach

prodded over on your back
Invulnerable hump
that stumped us

pincers prepare to
pick your secrets
bludgeons of light
to force your seams

Old fossil
glistening
in the continuous rain
of meteorites
blown to you from
between the stars
Stilt feet
mobilize to alight upon you
Ticking feelers
cracks   determine your fissures

to impact a pest
of electric eggs in the
cracks of your cold
volcanoes
Tycho Copernicus Kappa
look for geysers

strange abrasions
May Swenson   zodiacal wounds

Spacepoem 1:
from Laika to Gagarin

ra ke ta ra ke ta ra ke ta ra ke ta ra ke ta ra ke ta ra ke ta
sputsputsputsputsputsputsputsputsputsputsputsputsputsput
nik lai nik bel nik strel nik pchel nik mush nik chernush nik zvezdoch
kakakakakakakakakakakakakakakakakakakakakakakakakakakaka
spu spu tink spu kak spink spu sobak spu ka kink tak so
nikka laika kalai kanikka kanaka kana sput
nikka belka kabel kanikka kanaka kana stup
nikka strelka kastrel kanikka kanaka kana pust
nikka pchelka kapchel kanikka kanaka kana psut
nikka mushka kamush kanikka kanaka kana tusp
nikka chernushka kachernush kanikka kanaka kana tsup
nikka zvezdochka kazvezdoch kanikka kanaka kana upst
barker whitiearrow beespot blackie star
whitie arrowbarker beeblackie star spot
arrow barkerbee whitiestar blackie spot
bee arrowwhitie barkerspot star blackie
barkbark! whitewhitewhite! blackblackblackblack!
star! spot! sput! stop! star! sputsput! star! spout! psurt! start!
starrow! starrow! starrow!

putputputputputputputputputputputputputputputputputput
nikniknikniknikniknikniknikniknikniknikniknikniknikniknik
ka kra keta ka kra keta ka kra keta ka kra keta ka kra keta
kaktok kaktok kaktok kaktok kaktok kaktok kaktok kaktok
dakakvos dakakvos dakakvos dakakvos dakakvos dakakvos
davostok davostok davstok davostok davostok davostok davstok
dadadadadadadadadadadadadadadadadadadadadadadadadadada
daga daga daga daga daga daga daga daga daga daga daga
dagaga dagaga dagaga dagaga dagaga dagaga dagaga dagaga
dakakgaga rin dakakgaga rin dakakgaga rin dakakgaga rin
vostok! mir! vladi! yuri! mir! vladi! vladimir! vladivostok!
yurimirny! vladimirny! yurilaika! nikitaraketa! balalaika!
raketasobakaslava! vladislava!

Edwin Morgan

MOONWORDS

THE PLACE: Tranquility Base - a 'stark but beautiful' boulder-strewn wasteland on the right-hand side of the moon, in the Mare Tranquillitatis.

THE TIME: First quarter (moon), 3.52 a.m. July 21 (BST), 109.19.16 (Apollo mission time) - and the beginning of the moon age. Although we have provided a glossary some of the technical phrases will remain unclear to some readers. One day, no doubt, they will be common usage.

GLOSSARY OF TERMS

LEC Cable
LM Lunar Module
LOS Loss of Signal
MCC Mission Control Centre Houston
PAO NASA Public Affairs Officer
PLSS Portable Life Support System
RCU Remote Control Unit
SRC Sample Return Container
VESICLES Bubbles

PAO Neil Armstrong on the porch of the Eagle at 109 hours 19 minutes and 30 seconds to LOS, all systems go, over.

ARMSTRONG You need more slack, Buzz?

ALDRIN No, hold it just a minute.

ARMSTRONG Okay.

PAO 25 minutes of PLSS time expended.

ALDRIN Okay, everything's nice and sunny here.

ARMSTRONG Okay, can you pull the door open a little more?

MCC Roger, we copy and we're standing by for your TV.

ARMSTRONG Houston, this is
Neil. Radio check.
MCC Neil, this is Houston. You're
loud and clear. Break, break.
Buzz, this is Houston. Radio check
and verify TV circuit breaker in.
ALDRIN Roger, TV circuit
breaker in.
MCC Man, we're getting a picture
on the TV.
ALDRIN Oh, you got a good picture?
MCC There's a great deal of con-
trast in it and currently its upside
down on our monitor but we can
make out a fair amount of detail.
ALDRIN Okay, will you verify the
position: the opening I ought to
have on camera.
MCC Stand by. Okay Neil, we can
see you coming down the ladder now.
ARMSTRONG Okay, I just checked -
getting back to that first step,
Buzz. It's not even collapsed too
far but it's adequate to get back up.
It takes a pretty good little jump.
I'm at the foot of the ladder. The
LM footpads are only depressed
in the surface about one or two
inches. Although the surface
appears to be very finely grained
as you get close to it, it's almost
like a powder. Now and then it's
very fine. I'm going to step off
the LM now. That's one small

step for man, one giant leap for mankind. As the surface is fine and powdery, I can pick it up loosely with my toe. It does adhere in fine layers like powdered charcoal to the sole and sides of my boots. I can only go in a small fraction of an inch. Maybe an eighth of an inch, but I can see the footprints of my boots and the treads in the fine sandy particles. There seems to be no difficulty in moving around as we suspected. It's perhaps even easier than the simulations at one-sixth that we performed in the simulations on the ground. It's actually no trouble to walk around. The descent engine did not leave a crater of any size. There's about a foot clearance on the ground. We're essentially on a level place here - very level place here. I can see some evidence of rays emanating from the descent engine, but very insignificant amount. Okay, Buzz, we're ready to bring down the camera.

ALDRIN I'm all ready. I think it's been all squared away and in good shape. Okay. You'll have to pay out all the LEC. It looks like it's coming out nice and even.

ARMSTRONG Okay, it's quite

dark here in the shadow and a little hard for me to see if I have good footing. I'll work my way over into the sunlight here without directly looking into the sun.

ALDRIN Okay, it's taut now.

PAO Unofficial time on the first step 109. 24. 20.

ALDRIN Yes, I think it's pulling the wrong one.

ARMSTRONG Okay, I'm with you. Pull it down now. There was still a little bit left in the ...

ALDRIN Okay, don't hold it quite so tight. Okay?

ARMSTRONG Looking up at the LM. I'm standing directly in the shadow now. Looking up at Buzz in the shadow and I can see everything quite clearly. The light is sufficiently bright, backlighted into the front of the LM that everything is very clearly visible.

ALDRIN Okay.

PAO The surgeon says that the crew is doing well. Data is good.

ARMSTRONG I'll step out and take some of my first pictures here.

MCC Roger. Neil, we're reading you loud and clear. We see you getting some pictures and the contingency sample.

ALDRIN He's getting some pictures and the contingency sample.

PAO $35\frac{1}{2}$ minutes PLSS time expended now.

MCC This is Houston. Did you copy about the contingency sample? Over.

ARMSTRONG I'm going to get that just as soon as I finish these picture series.

ALDRIN Okay, going to get the contingency sample now, Neil?

ARMSTRONG Right. That's good. Okay, the contingency sample is down and it's (garbled). Looks like it's a little difficult to dig through ... This is very interesting. It's a very soft surface, but here and there, where I plug with the contingency sample collector, I run into a very hard cohesive material of the same sort. I'll try to get a rock in here. Here's a couple.

ALDRIN That looks beautiful from here, Neil.

ARMSTRONG It has a stark beauty all its own. It's like much of the high desert of the United States. It's different but it's very pretty out here. Be advised that a lot of the rock samples out here, the hard rock samples, have what appear to be vesicles in the surface. Also, I am looking at one now that appears to have some sort of phenocryst.

ALDRIN Container handle is off the ... In about six or eight inches of the (fade).

ARMSTRONG It is. It's ... I'm sure I could push it in further, but it's hard for me to bend down further than that.

ALDRIN Now, you can ...

ARMSTRONG You can really throw things a long way out there. That pocket open, Buzz?

ALDRIN Yes it is, but it's not up against your suit. Hit it back once more. More towards the inside. Okay, that's good.

ARMSTRONG That in the pocket?

ALDRIN Yes, push it down. Got it? No, it's not all the way in. Push it. There you go.

ARMSTRONG Contingency sample is in the pocket. I ... oxygen is 81 per cent. I have no flags and I'm in minimum flow.

ALDRIN Okay, I have got the cameras on at one frame a second. And I've got the 80 per cent. No flags.

ARMSTRONG Are you getting a TV picture now, Houston?

MCC Yes, Neil, we are getting a TV picture. Neil, this is Houston. We're getting a picture here. It's the first time we can see the bag

on the LEC being moved by Buzz, though. Here you come into our field of view.

ARMSTRONG Hold it a second. First, let me move that over the edge for you.

ALDRIN Okay. Are you ready for me to come out?

ARMSTRONG Yes. Just stand by a second. I'll move this over the handrail. Okay?

ALDRIN All right. That's got it. Are you ready?

ARMSTRONG All set. Okay, you saw what difficulties I was having. I'll try to watch your PLSS from underneath here.

ALDRIN All right. The backup camera is in position.

ARMSTRONG Okay, your PLSS is ... Looks like it is clearing okay. The shoes are about to come over the sill. Okay, now drop your PLSS down. There you go, you're clear and spiderly. You're good. About an inch clearance on top of your PLSS. Okay, you need a little bit of arching of the back to come down (garbled).

ALDRIN How far are my feet from the ... ?

ARMSTRONG Okay, you ... you're right at the edge of the porch, Buzz.

Okay, your back in ... a little of
foot movement ... Little arching of
the back. Hope it comes up and
cleared the bulkhead without any
trouble at all. Looks good.

PAO 45 minutes PLSS time
expended.

MCC Neil, this is Houston. Based
on your camera transfer. Do you
foresee any difficulties in SRC
transfer? Over.

ARMSTRONG Negative.

PAO It's the sample return containers,
the rock boxes that MCC ...

ALDRIN Now I want to back up and
partially close the hatch, making
sure not to lock it on my way out.

ARMSTRONG A good thought.

ALDRIN That's our home for the
next couple of hours and I want to
take good care of it. Okay, I'm
on the top step and I can look down
over the RCU landing gear pads.
That's a very simple matter to hop
down from one step to the next.

ARMSTRONG Yes, I found it to be
very comfortable and walking is
also very comfortable. You've got
three more steps and then a long
one.

ALDRIN Okay, I'm going to leave
that one foot up there and both hands
down to about the fourth rung up.

ARMSTRONG There you go.

ALDRIN Okay, now I think I'll do
the same.

ARMSTRONG A little more. About
another inch. There, you got it.
That's a good step. About a
three-footer.

ALDRIN Beautiful, beautiful.

Off Course

the golden flood	the weightless seat
the cabin song	the pitch black
the growing beard	the floating crumb
the shining rendezvous	the orbit wisecrack
the hot space	the smuggled mouth-organ
the imaginary somersault	the visionary sunrise
the tuning continents	the space debris
the golden lifeline	the space walk
the crawling deltas	the camera moon
the pitch velvet	the rough sleep
the crackling headphone	the space silence
the turning earth	the lifeline continents
the cabin sunrise	the hot flood
the shining spacesuit	the growing moon
the crackling somersault	the smuggled orbit
the rough moon	the visionary rendezvous
the weightless headphone	the cabin debris
the floating lifeline	the pitch sleep
the crawling camera	the turning silence
the space crumb	the crackling beard
the orbit mouth-organ	the floating song

Edwin Morgan

This subway station

This subway station
with its electric lights, pillars of steel, arches of cement,
    and trains -
quite an improvement on the caves of the caveman;
but, look! on this wall
a primitive drawing.

Charles Reznikoff

Acknowledgements   For permission to use copyright material acknowledgement is made to the
following:

Poems and Prose   For 'Found Poem' by Jean L'Anselme (previously 'found' by Gerard Hoffnung)
translated by Michael Benedikt from *The Ring Around the World* to Rapp &
Whiting Ltd; for 'Repairing a Joint' from *Sabotage at the Forge* by Richard
Armstrong to the author and J. M. Dent & Sons Ltd; for 'The Mechanical
Hound' from *Farenheit 451* by Ray Bradbury to A. D. Peters & Co. and
Harold Matson Co. Inc.; for 'Used Trout Stream' from *The Cleveland Wrecking
Yard* by Richard Brautigan to the Grove Press Inc.; for 'Pig at Machine' from
Smallcreep's Day by Peter C. Brown to the author and Victor Gollancz Ltd;
for 'The Principle of the Helicopter' from *The Notebooks of Leonardo da Vinci*
translated by E. McCurdy to Jonathan Cape Ltd; for 'Life in the Machine'
from 'The Machine Stops' from *The Collected Short Stories of E. M. Forster*
to the author and Sidgwick & Jackson Ltd; for 'Carving a Goldfish' by Ian
Griffiths to the author; for 'Frogman' by Seamus Heaney to the author; for
'The Easter Islanders Show Thor Heyerdahl How One of Their Giant Statues
Was Moved' from *Aku Aku* by Thor Heyerdahl to the author and George Allen
& Unwin Ltd; for 'Wings' by Miroslav Holub translated by George Theiner
from *Selected Poems* to Penguin Books Ltd; for 'The Bugmobile' by David
Karliner to the author and *Drive*; for 'Mining Rhyming' by William Keating
from *Folk Song in England* by A. L. Lloyd to the author; for 'The Ballad of the
Big Hewer' by Ewan MacColl from *The Radio Ballads*, prepared for BBC Radio,
to Ewan MacColl and Charles Parker, music by Peggy Seeger; for 'Plastecine
Sculpture' by Alice McKeown to the author; for 'I Like That Stuff' from *Poems*
by Adrian Mitchell to the author and Jonathan Cape Ltd; for 'The Computer's
Second Christmas Card', 'Construction for Isambard Kingdom Brunel',
'O Pioneers!', 'Space Poem 1: from Laika to Gagarin' and 'A View of Things'
from *The Second Life* by Edwin Morgan to the author and the Edinburgh
University Press; for 'How to Find Heath Robinson' and 'Off Course' by Edwin
Morgan to the author; for 'The Picket Fence from *Gallows Songs* by Christian
Morgenstern translated by Max Knight to the author and the University of
California Press; for 'Spit Nolan' from *The Goalkeeper's Revenge and Other
Stories* by Bill Naughton to George G. Harrap & Co. Ltd; for 'Coal-Mine'
from *The Road to Wigan Pier* by George Orwell to Miss Sonia Brownell and
Secker & Warburg Ltd; for 'News' from *Close the Coalhouse Door* by Alan
Plater to the author and Methuen & Co. Ltd; for 'The Little Giant' from
The Golden Age of Steam by John Pudney to the author and Hamish Hamilton
Ltd; for 'The Last Great Tram Race' by Philip Purser to the *Daily Telegraph*;
for 'This subway station' from *By the Waters of Manhattan* by Charles
Reznikoff to the author and New Directions Publishing Corporation; for
'Who do you think you are?' from *The People, Yes* by Carl Sandburg, 'Jug'
from *Smoke and Steel* by Carl Sandburg and 'The Makers of Speed' from

Index of Authors, Translators and Collectors